Romantic STYLE

Romantic **STYLE**

Selina Lake
& SARA NORRMAN

PHOTOGRAPHY BY DEBI TRELOAR

RYLAND PETERS & SMALL
LONDON • NEW YORK

Styling Selina Lake
Text Sara Norrman

Senior designer Megan Smith
Designer Julie Bennett
Commissioning editor Annabel Morgan
Editor Nathan Joyce
Location research Jess Walton and
    Selina Lake
Head of production Patricia Harrington
Art director Leslie Harrington
Editorial director Julia Charles

First published in 2010
This edition published in 2014
by Ryland Peters and Small
20–21 Jockey's Fields
London WC1R 4BW
and
519 Broadway, 5th Floor
New York, NY 10012

www.rylandpeters.com

10 9 8 7 6 5 4 3 2 1

ISBN: 978 1 84975 510 8

A CIP record for this book is
available from the British Library.

Library of Congress Cataloging-in-
Publication Data

This book was previously catalogued
as follows:

Lake, Selina.
    Romantic style/Selina Lake
& Sara Norrman ; photography
by Debi Treloar.
    -- 1st ed.
    p. cm.
    Includes index.
    ISBN 978-1-84975-040-0
1. Interior decoration--Psychological
aspects. I. Norrman, Sara. II.
Treloar, Debi. III. Title.
    NK2113.L35 2010
    747.01'9--dc22
                        2010015198

Printed and bound in China

contents

Introduction

With its soft tones, mellow mood and hints of nostalgia, the romantic style creates a home that's warm and welcoming. You could say it's the interiors equivalent of the Slow Food movement – instead of rushing to a shop and buying a whole room set, you slowly, over time, build up a collection of things you love.

The romantic style is in tune with the times. After a hard-hitting recession, many of us are eschewing a frenzied consumerist lifestyle and turning to more sustainable sources of shopping, such as car boot/yard sales, flea markets and auctions and antiques shops. We are also getting savvier when it comes to reusing furniture and recycling old items, giving them fresh life via restoration or even finding new uses for them.

This book shows how you can turn your space into a romantic haven, offering you pages filled with images of beautiful, seductive rooms. But reality checks such as a large family, your partner's decorating taste or living in rented accommodation might stop you from following the style to the letter. If this is the case, then use this book as a source of inspiration for those parts of your home that could do with a touch of romance – perhaps a shelf in the bathroom that's all yours, a section of the bedroom where you can show off your best-loved shoes or a mantelpiece adorned with flowers and candles.

While this is a style full of frills, fabrics and florals, there are aspects that will appeal to even hardened modernists. When you pare away all the details, romantic style is one of the most important aspects of interior design – falling in love with your home.

Romantic inspirations

Vintage pieces make welcome additions to almost any Romantic Style scheme, but while some rooms blend both old and new for a modern romantic feel, others unashamedly plunder the past for an out-and-out vintage look that glories in the elegant lines, subtle hues and quirky charm of centuries-old design.

Vintage romantic

ABOVE LEFT *Fresh flowers are a staple of the vintage romantic look and this antique bust seems to peep out from among the blooms.*

LEFT *Vintage pieces lend themselves to decorative arrangements. Here, old hardbacks with faded jackets are stacked next to a simple bouquet to create an understated mantelpiece display.*

OPPOSITE *A true vintage romantic scheme, complete with antique sofas, a dramatic mirror and elegant china. Shutters are a simpler window treatment than curtains and don't compete with the striking furniture in this room.*

Romantic style is far removed from spare modern aesthetics – it's the complete antidote to bare spaces accessorized with careful groupings of minimalist modern furniture. And so it feels natural to look to vintage and antique pieces to furnish a romantic home. But you don't need to invest in fine antiques to create this facet of the romantic look – a worn sideboard or scuffed chest of drawers is far better suited to the vintage romantic look than an expensive Louis XIV chair.

The vintage romantic look is to a large extent centred around nostalgia. It harks back to days gone by; days we like to look back on through a rose-tinted haze. Thankfully, finding pieces that evoke the past is fairly easy. Flea markets, car boot/yard sales and junk shops

OPPOSITE *With its calming colour scheme and use of fabrics, this welcoming living room has an inviting and cosy feel. The linen cover on the sofa works as a great foil to the multicoloured vintage cushions. Using unframed pictures helps to keep the scheme simple and prevents* *it from becoming overloaded. It's important not to add too much clutter or create a fussy effect when using vintage items.* **LEFT** *Old-fashioned lampshades adorned with tassels and embroidery are a great way to introduce a feeling of days gone by, but keeping the scheme soft and pale* *ensures the effect isn't overwhelming.* **ABOVE** *Using fresh blooms in a room keeps it fragrant. Add a witty touch by stacking vintage lampshades to create an instant talking point – experiment with using things in creative ways to establish a style that's uniquely your own.*

are piled high with old oil paintings, tasselled lampshades, retro fabrics and unrestored chandeliers. And such items are real treasure when it comes to the vintage romantic style.

Paintings often go for a song at auctions and flea markets and are an overlooked source of romantic styling. The trick is to see beyond the stacks of amateurish daubs and sort the wheat from the chaff. First of all, trust your gut instinct. If you like a painting, for whatever reason, go for it – styling is often about finding a common ground and a relationship between pieces, whether that be a colour, a texture or simply your own taste.

When grouping pictures, you can also make them work if you arrange them by colour. Hang paintings with similar, calm tones together, and they will look coherent even if they have very different subject matters. Avoiding ornate frames and keeping things simple can also bring a look together. If you love the gilded opulence of old picture frames, remove the paintings and hang them empty. Against a pale wall, such frames can create a beautiful and intriguing display.

Keeping background colours simple is a good trick when you have lots of vintage pieces. After all, you want to create a cosy haven with retro hints, rather than conjure up the feel of your grandmother's house. If you're lucky enough to have two or three beautiful old cushions, make sure they're displayed on a sofa covered in simple, unpatterned fabric. And if you collect old paintings, hang them on a wall painted a quiet shade, to avoid too many conflicting patterns and shades.

A sense of humour is a handy tool when searching for vintage items. One little porcelain dog or shepherdess might not look interesting all alone, but group a collection of similar items together and display them against a simple background or on top of a white-painted chest, and they'll take on an added dimension. In the same way, one vintage lampshade might seem unassuming, but a teetering pile of them stacked together will raise a smile. It's all about experimenting, daring to think outside the box and finding new ways to use old things.

Antique clothes and accessories are often decorative enough to be kept permanently on display, hanging from dado rails, decorative screens or other pieces of furniture. Concentrate on the shade and fabric rather than the shape of a garment – you might never actually wear it, but you'll see it every day. One brightly coloured dress or top can provide inspiration for a whole room scheme, while fabrics such as chiffon and silk can be echoed in your choice of curtains and cushions.

Vintage accessories provide an instant hit of girly romance, especially creamy pearl

OPPOSITE LEFT *Vivid colours work well in a romantic interior. Here, bubblegum-pink walls have been teamed with curtains in an equally vivid fuchsia, making the whole room pop.*

OPPOSITE RIGHT *Old chandeliers with drops missing can be customized with your own personal treasures, whatever they might be here, some decorative feathered birds are perching happily among the dangling crystals.*

RIGHT *A heavy cast-iron fire surround is lightened up with the addition of a pretty blouse, some glass votive holders and fresh flowers. Hiding away the shoes you love is a shame, so show off their elegant shapes even when you're not wearing them.*

BELOW *Beloved vintage and new dresses are proudly displayed together to provide an instant hit of colour. A pretty display like this is easy to change when the mood takes you.*

LEFT *A careful grouping of feathers, silk flowers and vintage jewels makes a dressmaker's dummy into a decorative feature. It's also easy to change when you feel inspired – follow the seasons with a vintage tippet in winter and luscious fabric flowers for summer.*

Vintage romantic 17

necklaces and jet brooches. Drape strings of beads over dressmaker's dummies, pour them into glass bowls or sling them over a mirror – any way you use them, such accessories will instantly soften a room.

You can often find a wide variety of glass and ceramic pieces in antiques shops, from champagne coupes to decorative side plates. Pick up pieces that appeal to you. A single beautiful glass might not be of much use if you're throwing a party, but collect them over time, then arrange them on a windowsill for an eye-catching display.

Vintage plates look great en masse, but stick to a single theme or colour, whether it be patterns taken from nature or a specific shade of blue. This will make the plates gel beautifully when they are grouped together on a wall or just arranged decoratively on a side table.

ABOVE *The delicate blues and golds of these plates ensure they match, and the theme of birds, foliage and flowers unites them further. Start with one plate and build a collection from there, sticking to a theme to keep it coherent.*

OPPOSITE *Romantic certainly doesn't have to mean pink. Dark, rich tones can also create a wonderful mood, as demonstrated by this moody indigo hallway. Try painting the woodwork, radiators and window frames the same shade to keep the scheme calm despite its rich tones. A metal artwork on a stand is glammed up by a few strands of crystals, while a table lamp in glossy bronze adds shimmer and pizzazz.*

Simple romantic

Romantic style needn't be frilly, pink or frivolous. Instead, pale colours, simple lines and subtle metallic accents can create a look that's relaxed and cool yet still evokes a sense of romance. Keep walls and floors pale and interesting to offset your furniture, and let the fabrics and accessories create the mood.

ABOVE *An embroidered shawl on a plain background can be prettier than a picture. Three-dimensional objects on a white wall often have more impact than prints.*

RIGHT *For a spot in your home that rests both body and soul, keep lines uncluttered and the scheme simple. The grouping of framed mirrors is easy to recreate — just paint old frames white, then rub them down for a distressed look. Ask a glazier to cut mirrors to size and you have a great-looking display that also helps a room look bigger.*

THIS PAGE *An old chest of drawers is given extra romance with a clutch of pretty pieces arranged on top. Shutters keep the look clean and unfussy. The artwork is made from an old lace tablecloth, stretched across a canvas and sealed with a wash of plaster.*

OPPOSITE *A carefully thought-out and deliberately uncluttered display of beautiful pieces sits on this mantelpiece, including a picture frame made from an old ceiling tile salvaged in New York. Reflective and sparkly surfaces lift the otherwise all-white scheme.*

Simple needn't equal boring. This take on the romantic look combines simple shapes, tactile fabrics and worn materials with flair, and pulling the different elements together is the absence of busy patterns and colours.

The key to this look is white, but not the brilliant, dazzling variety. Instead, think of whites with undertones of grey, pink or cream. It's fascinating how the white spectrum ranges from harsh, clinical whites with a blue base note to a warm, almost peachy shade. Invest in sample-size tins of your six favourite white paints, apply each shade to a large piece of paper, then compare the colours in situ on your walls. Remember to study the shades at various different times of day, as they will look very different in daylight and beneath electric light. Whichever white takes your fancy, make sure it has a subtle hint of nostalgia about it — it's the softer effect of aged paint you're after, rather than the hard, dazzling finish of a freshly painted white wall.

Team your chosen shade with natural flooring — wooden floorboards, perhaps, or sisal matting. The mix of textures and the simplicity of the natural materials will sit comfortably with the pale walls and with any vintage accessories you choose to go with it.

To prevent white from becoming cold and sterile, marry it up with pieces that have soul.

If you're in the market for a new mirror, don't just take the easy option and head for the local shopping mall. Instead, hunt around for a vintage example. Old mirrors have seen a few things in their lives, and their tarnished silver frames and aged patina will bring soul and romance to any interior.

When it comes to creating interest in a pale interior, texture is important. For the living room it's worth investing in a soft rug

BELOW The colours in this bedroom keep the scheme cool and tasteful. Curtains in a luxurious silk fabric add a touch of glamour to a boudoir, and the matching fabric lampshade proves it's a well thought through scheme. Layering matching bed linen adds to the sumptuous effect.

to pull the interior together. Rug companies have come a long way in recent years, and you're sure to find whatever style, colour and size you want after a quick trawl on the internet. If you're after something specific, there are companies that will create bespoke floor coverings to your very own design.

Transparent or reflective surfaces can also contribute to a simple look. Introduce glass in the shape of a collection of carafes or vases on a windowsill. Chandeliers twinkle gently when lit and cast drops of light across a room via their multifaceted crystals. Perspex/Plexiglass and other transparent plastics have become fashionable in the past few years, and design classics such as Kartell's Bourgie light add instant impact to a room. Perspex/Plexiglass sideboards, chairs and coffee tables are widely available, and work especially well if you have decided to go for that extra-special rug – what's the point of investing in a beautiful floor covering if it's hidden beneath a mahogany coffee table?

Of course, you can use colour in the simple romantic home. But steer clear of deep, intense shades. Pastels can also be tricky, as if they are too sugary they'll make whites look washed out. Instead, think of clear blues and fresh reds that have faded over the years, like patterns on old porcelain tea sets. Floral patterns like those on Aubusson rugs and sprigged country-garden prints also work well, but avoid geometrics or futuristic forms.

THIS PAGE *Restricting yourself to a palette of muted, calm shades allows you to combine items that otherwise might not sit comfortably together. The simple lines of these sofas keep the room uncluttered, and the rumpled cushions and throws ensure things stay casual. Textures are important in white rooms, and here the rug, the transparent lamp and the leather pouffe work wonders in creating visual interest.*

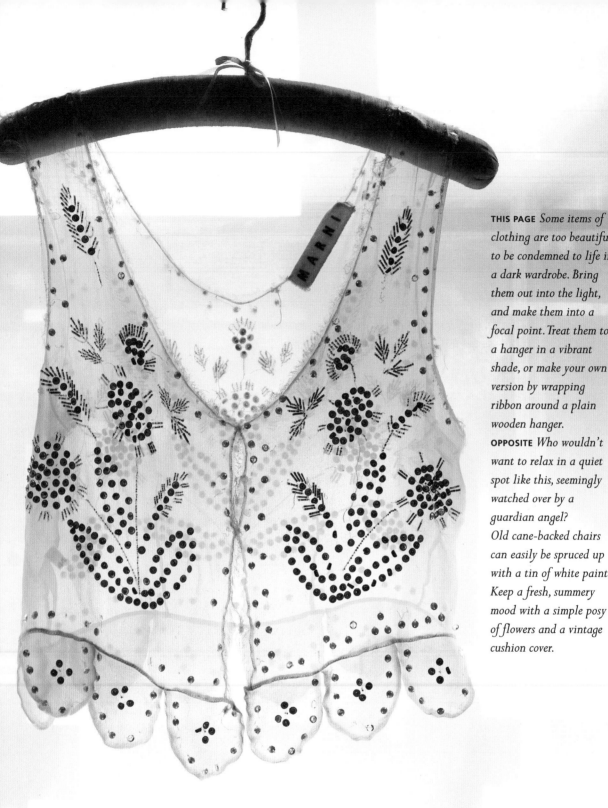

THIS PAGE *Some items of clothing are too beautiful to be condemned to life in a dark wardrobe. Bring them out into the light, and make them into a focal point. Treat them to a hanger in a vibrant shade, or make your own version by wrapping ribbon around a plain wooden hanger.*

OPPOSITE *Who wouldn't want to relax in a quiet spot like this, seemingly watched over by a guardian angel? Old cane-backed chairs can easily be spruced up with a tin of white paint. Keep a fresh, summery mood with a simple posy of flowers and a vintage cushion cover.*

While most of us love a clean, uncluttered look, the reality of a home is often very different. We all have to live with books, clothes, toys, paperwork, sports gear and all the other bits of paraphernalia we accumulate as we move through life. And there's nothing wrong with that, as long as storage is well planned. In fact, an all-white scheme can trick the eye into ignoring functional storage units or sideboards, instead drawing it along white floors, up past the storage and on to an interesting display on the walls, for example.

An all-white look also allows us to display collections that could create a rather chaotic and less coherent impression if the items were in a multitude of different colours. And opting for a single colour in a room also allows you to boldly mix up furniture from a variety of different eras, from funky Sixties lamps to Art Deco-inspired pieces and old Victorian mirrors. Monochrome schemes are a great unifying agent, as well as a fail-safe way to produce a simple home that still feels romantic, warm and welcoming.

RIGHT *This extensive collection of cream ceramics is held together by its monochrome theme. The rug, by designer Tracey Boyd, provides a foil for the sleek Art Deco-style dining table and chairs, while the lamp on the sideboard is a Sixties design. The pale scheme is broken up by the use of natural tongue and groove cladding on the wall.*

Elegant romantic

Soothing shades and curvaceous lines that are reminiscent of another era come together for the most elegant of the romantic inspirations. The colours are deliberately faded and subdued to offset the embellished and intricate shapes of the furniture, while hints of gilding and antique silver add lustre to the scheme.

ABOVE *If you're lucky enough to have inherited beads or baubles that feel a bit old-fashioned for daily wear, display them in glass bowls instead.*
RIGHT *Items from several different eras can be found here, from the Rococo-style side chairs to a 1940s floor lamp. The calm tones and touches of dull metal hold the scheme together and create an elegantly simple setting.*

If creating a vintage look means scouring car boot/yard sales for second-hand furniture, then giving it a facelift with a lick of paint, the elegant romantic look demands a little more effort. The lines of the furniture borrow from such styles as Rococo and Neo-classicism, with hints of Empire and the Baroque. But to prevent your home looking like a museum, mixing up the eras while keeping fabrics and colours simple is an easy way to ensure a relaxed mood.

Hints of sophistication can be added via accessories – items with historical connotations, such as globes, chandeliers and majestic floor-standing candelabras, are quick ways to impart a sense of elegance. And you don't have to spend vast amounts of money in antiques emporiums either. Look out for stone statuettes in garden centres – when brought indoors and placed on a pedestal or side table, they'll take on a whole new role.

Antique books are another way to add old-world charm. Thick, leather-bound tomes with gilded pages can be found in second-hand bookshops for not a lot of money, especially if you're not too concerned about the state of the actual pages within. But beware – you don't want to achieve that uniform, fake frontage look with row upon row of books that aren't intended to be read. Love your antique books for what they are – historic items in their own right – but don't be afraid to display them alongside your well-thumbed paperbacks. It's this mix of the useful and the beautiful that gives any home a sense of soul.

ABOVE *Plain bowls and classic cutlery can be found in most department stores, and look timeless when paired with traditional roses.*
BELOW *The faded silver of these candlesticks gives a hint of elegant nostalgia, and works wonders beside white flowers. Inexpensive items like this silvered ball can also look great in the right setting.*

OPPOSITE *The tall windows let light flow into this elegant space – it's hard to believe the whole apartment consists of only one room. There's a mixture of natural materials, from a coffee table made from rough planks of driftwood to the giant shell on the deep windowsill. An embroidered piano shawl embellishes the mezzanine railings, while two antique doors are beautiful enough to be displayed as artworks.*

Elegant romantic 33

All types of candlelight are important in romantic schemes, but for the ultimate in elegance choose tall, slender candlesticks in a period style – tiny tealights just don't cut the mustard when placed on a beautifully arranged, formal dinner table. Old silver candlesticks reflect the light beautifully, but avoid shiny new silver. The dulled reflections of tarnished silver give off a much more romantic sheen, and it's also worth looking out for pewter, brass and iron versions as well.

Victorian cast-iron candelabras in various states of disrepair can often be sourced cheaply in junk shops, and are well worth snapping up. Clean off any rust with sandpaper, then get creative with spray paint – the ornate shapes will ensure that the candelabra looks elegant, while a fresh coat of paint will keep it looking informal.

You don't need a palatial home or a grandiose space to achieve this look – even a tiny studio flat can be decidedly elegant. Stick to simple, soft colours on the walls, floors and ceilings – pearly greys, stone and creamy whites, perhaps – highlighted by metallic accents and natural textures. Furniture can come from all eras and all corners of the globe, but must be rather cosily well worn to create the required effect of faded grandeur. To continue the romantic mood, conceal ugly reminders of the modern world such as the television, entertainment system, telephone and computer and their inevitable tangle of electrical leads. Tucking them all away requires planning and calls for ingenious storage systems, but when it's done it's surprising how relaxing a technology-free room can be.

Textiles are very important when it comes to giving visual clues as to which historical era you're inspired by.

OPPOSITE ABOVE *An ornately carved bedhead makes an elegant statement. Thankfully, plenty of companies now make modern versions of antique beds, as the older versions are often lacking in the comfort stakes.*

OPPOSITE BELOW *Different floral patterns can be teamed effectively, just as long as the background colours are kept the same. Here, the beige linen stops the patterns from feeling frumpy or staid.*

THIS PAGE *The white-on-white embroidery on these vintage textiles makes both an elegant and subtle impact. Pile up white bed linen in a variety of different textures to stop it from looking clinical.*

THIS PAGE *Vintage dresses are layered with beads and scarves, while the dried roses are part of the owner's bridal bouquet — it just doesn't get more romantic than that!*

LEFT *Even a forgotten niche can become a thing of beauty when items are grouped thoughtfully. Here, a fragment of a moulding that probably came from a fire surround has been painted a similar shade to the two old candle holders. An armful of dried leaves is displayed in a simple jug, while a selection of vintage frames have been sprayed a calming silver shade.*

Heavy brocades and embroidered satin instantly take you back to the splendours of the court of Louis XVI, while simpler stitches and muslins evoke Jane Austen heroines gossiping over their needlework. Reworking fabrics and textiles into new items can be hugely rewarding. If you find a square of fine embroidery that isn't quite big enough to cover a cushion, stitch it onto a piece of linen instead, for a look that's both classic and modern at the same time. Old French linen is often of good enough quality to cover sofas and chairs with, and can be tracked down on French eBay, if you first arm yourself with a few stock phrases. Old silk curtains and drapes may be bleached by the sun, but when any faded bits are trimmed off they make for sumptuous bed

BELOW *Simple white cotton fabric has been used to create a fun and frilly lampshade and matching cushion cover. The wire frame sofa was originally intended for the garden, but keeps the room feeling light and airy. The large frames leaning against the wall are all painted the same colour, and don't need pictures in them to create a great display.*

RIGHT *Even with a decommissioned fireplace, you can still create a romantic ambience with a simple string of mini lights. Add a cluster of votive holders on the mantelpiece, reflected in a pretty mirror. The glossy surfaces of glass or metallic ornaments, vases and jugs will help to cast fragments of light around the room.*

linen. In short, any vintage material that catches your fancy can be reworked and given new life, if you only look at it through creative eyes.

When it comes to greenery, less is definitely more for the elegant look. White flowers of all descriptions always come across as classically beautiful, while branches of eucalyptus, trailing twigs of ivy and single blooms will also fit the bill. But remember to keep your flowers looking loose and artlessly thrown together, rather than stiff or over-arranged – the stately home look might work in an authentic setting, but it's probably not a style you'd like to live with at home.

LEFT *Setting dark wood vintage furniture against an all-white scheme lets it breathe and keeps the look light and modern. Using bold spots of contemporary colour like the turquoise lampshade also gives a fresh impression. A chandelier finishes off the romantic look, while the Roman blinds are clean and pared back in contrast.*

BELOW *Grouping glass candlesticks creates an elegant still life. Choose zingy green and purple candles rather than the obvious white ones to add an extra layer of interest. The portrait on the wall has been left unframed to make it look less fussy.*

Modern romantic

Contemporary furniture and simple lines can be used to great effect in a romantic scheme. With a few touches, even the most modern of homes can be turned into a softer, more welcoming space, whether you live in a grand Victorian villa or a new build with few original features. It's all about having the courage to combine cutting-edge tones with bold decorative shapes, or mixing 1960s chairs with slinky silks — anything goes, as long as you follow a few basic rules.

THIS PAGE *The collection of colourful cushions on the sofa works well with the unusual light behind it, which is a Sixties original and is vaguely reminiscent of an orange flying saucer — very space age.*

THIS PAGE *This modern table is topped with a sheet of vibrant green glass that echoes the wings of the birds in the pretty wallpaper. The chairs are contemporary, but blend in well with the retro vases, vintage mirror and flowers. The magnificent roses are actually fake, but no less beautiful for that.*

If you've been struck by a longing to soften up your living space after decades of strict minimalist trends, you might feel dejected at the prospect of getting rid of your modular sofas or space-age chairs. But there's no need to start from scratch just because you hanker after a prettier place to live. There are plenty of ways to use those much-loved pieces of furniture that you've amassed over the years in a softer, more romantic scheme.

Accessories are the key to creating a modern romantic look. Start by softening up your rooms with the three staples: pretty fabrics, fresh flowers and atmospheric lighting. Cover a sleek sofa in pastel-tinted cushions and strokeable throws; heap a glass and metal dining table with bunches of peonies, roses and wild flowers (anything that isn't architectural and spiky). Light as many tealights as possible, hang chandeliers and group different-coloured candles in glass holders on streamlined modern sideboards. None of these things costs the earth, and all will add instant glamour and softness.

Many 20th-century design classics such as Alvar Aalto chairs and Saarinen tables have organic shapes that were groundbreaking when they were introduced, but which now feel surprisingly accessible. They seem to have come full circle, and can be teamed with the kind of traditional accessories their creators were striving to get away from – perhaps it's the greatest sign of good design that it sits so comfortably with so many different styles.

ABOVE *This Saarinen table and chairs were as cutting edge as they came when designed in the mid-1950s, but here the setting is warm and soft rather than futuristic, thanks to the addition of gilded candelabras, an antique mirror and a piano shawl with a sensuously fringed edge.*

Using funky furniture in a softer, more feminine setting can also prove a way out of the potential conflict zone that is cohabitation. Merging two tastes in one household is seldom easy, especially if one party has a predilection for cool contemporary pieces, while the other wants to cover every inch of their new home with silks, frills, scented candles and scatter cushions. In fact, the modern romantic scheme is almost the interiors equivalent of a marriage

THIS PAGE *The boxy lines of the white four-poster and the strictly stylized blooms of the wallpaper stops this bedroom from looking sugary sweet. Restricting the bed linen to one colour also emphasizes the upwardly climbing wallpaper, making the walls seem taller. Flower power never goes out of fashion.*

OPPOSITE *The retro flavour of the Love print by Robert Indiana is enforced by the embroidered top, while the hydrangeas on the balcony prove that you can have your own outdoor oasis no matter how small the space.*

guidance counsellor, encouraging
compromise without either party giving
up on their personal taste!

Keeping colour schemes pale and chic is
a sure-fire way of creating a modern feel, as
is ensuring that surfaces and walls are kept
uncluttered. You can introduce a romantic
mood by choosing pieces of furniture with
traditional roots that have been reworked
in contemporary form, such as four-poster
beds with pared-down lines, or sideboards
that nod to old styles but come in modern,
glossy finishes. Many designers are now
reworking classic styles and putting their

own spin on them – John Reeves' popular series of occasional tables and sideboards, for example, or Philippe Starck's ubiquitous Louis Ghost chair in clear Perspex/Plexiglass. Even Ikea has latched on to this trend with a four-poster bed that's almost minimal in its simple lines, and a sideboard that nods to the Baroque but comes in an eye-popping yellow gloss.

Colour is an easy way of adding a dash of cutting-edge style to a modern romantic scheme. Look out for on-trend, up-to-the-minute shades in brochures from paint manufacturers and in interiors magazines, then decide whether you want to update a single wall in your home, or to make over old furniture with a quick lick of paint.

If you want to set a trend rather than follow one, look to the latest catwalk reports, as colour trends often start there and break through in interiors a couple of seasons later. If you fall head over heels with a brash magenta or vivid green shade, make sure the item you plan to paint falls within the 'romantic' spectrum: the more fashion-forward the shade, the prettier the object should be. An intricately carved mahogany sideboard can look stunning in a punchy pink, while wooden kitchen chairs will take on a new lease of life when painted blistering yellow.

Romantic patterns are also making a comeback. Designers are rediscovering the joys of florals, but giving them more stylized appeal. Remember that bigger is often better when it comes to pattern, especially in small spaces – nothing makes a small room feel more claustrophobic than a tiny sprigged pattern. Think of the gigantic blossoms of Marimekko or the stylized twigs of Jocelyn Warner's patterns, and you'll be on the right track.

TOP *The modern shade of chartreuse brings this wall up to date, while the flowers add colour and shape.*
ABOVE *Pick up mismatched wooden kitchen chairs at flea markets and make them bang on trend with neon pink paint – any colour will work, as long as it's loud enough!*
OPPOSITE *Black on black can be stunning – just make sure you offset the dark wall and headboard with a glorious accent like this silk cushion.*

Romantic styling

Choosing colours that appeal can be daunting. Our eyes are trained to search for matching shades and shapes, rather than alighting upon hues that speak to us for emotional reasons. Try to shed your inhibitions and follow your gut instinct when it comes to colour — like taste and scent, the right shade will evoke memories that you thought were long forgotten. And don't ever worry about what 'goes'. If you like it, it works — it's as simple as that.

Colour

OPPOSITE *Gather together pieces that are visually pleasing to you due to their design, colour or pattern. Group them together in a temporary still life to create an inspirational display that may then influence a whole decorative scheme — take a quick snap of the tableau to act as a visual reminder.*

ABOVE LEFT *Squares of vintage wallpaper have been stuck together in a patchwork design on the wall behind a simple four-poster bed. If you feel nervous about plumping for such a riot of colours, find a common denominator like a single shade or type of pattern to make it all come together.*

ABOVE CENTRE *A faded advertising placard has been given a shot of colour in the shape of a vibrant red dress.*

ABOVE RIGHT *Warm, peachy tones will create a soothing and mellow feeling in a bedroom, but make sure you keep on the soft, faded side of the spectrum and avoid anything shiny and brash.*

CLOCKWISE FROM TOP LEFT *A vintage dress hanging on a cupboard is beautiful in its own right, whether you wear it or not. Painted MDF panels create instant colour and impact behind an old French bed, and are easy to take with you when you move — perfect if you are living in rented accommodation. Tall glass jars filled with unexpected items such as vintage cotton reels and hollow eggshells have a feeling of a Victorian curiosity cabinet. Books bought for their faded colours and bound with twine exude an air of nostalgia. A paper garland coiled in a simple glass jar looks sweet — try it with fairy lights. An old green suitcase set against a dusky pink wall serves no purpose at all other than to delight the eye.*

THIS PAGE *The plump cushions in powder-puff pink add a hint of retro romance. Gathering together several table lamps in different colours and sizes creates a theatrical effect and they look fabulous when they're all lit. Grouping items en masse adds impact to a room and works for everything from lamps to frames.*

THIS PAGE *Bubblegum pink works a treat in this room with its tall windows. The diaphanous silk curtains add a sumptous note. On the table, roses in orange, yellow and pink come together in an exotic medley, but their similar shapes and sizes stop them from looking messy. The table between the sofas is unusually high, but if you spend a lot of time eating, writing or playing games in your living room, this might be a better solution than a low table.*

ABOVE *This little bird and garland of flowers provide the finishing touches to a tea party.*
RIGHT *A vintage lamp takes on a quirky look against the bold pink.*

When asked what their favourite colour is, the majority of people will suggest the ubiquitous blue or green. Some might go as far as to mention mimosa yellow or lipstick red, but very few are as precise as 'the colour of the sea on holiday' or 'the pink of my first girlfriend's dress'. Yet it's precisely these shades that evoke an emotional response and that we might like to be reminded of on an everyday basis.

Interiors magazines talk about creating a mood board when you are planning a decorative scheme for your home, but all too often that entails looking for a specific wallpaper, fabric swatch or paint chart. It might prove more useful to create a still life of treasured photographs, items of clothing, paintings and books to get a feel for exactly what you like and why. Rummage through your wardrobe and pull out clothes that bring back happy memories; flick through photos

and search for moods you want to capture, and rifle through your CD collection or bookshelves for beautiful covers that inspire you. When you place all these items together, a pattern might start to emerge – a certain pale blue that jumped out from an old CD cover might also be repeated in the sky shown in your holiday snaps, and would look great in the guest bathroom (just don't tell your partner it's also the exact colour of your first boyfriend's eyes…).

Just as most of us can say roughly which colours we like, we are also quite set in our ways about what we don't like. Maybe the thought of having a bright pink dining room sets your teeth on edge, but when you see an inspiring image of one, your opinion might change. So when flicking through interiors magazines and design books, be open-minded and live by the rule that there are no rules!

OPPOSITE *Colours completely create the mood in this room. The chairs were painted with fluorescent pink paint, which can be bought in specialist shops. The window frames are a strong charcoal, which works as a foil to the pink. The windows are dressed with panels of lace stapled to frames for an updated version of net curtains.*

RIGHT AND FAR RIGHT *Fresh, zingy greens make this bedroom feel bold and modern, but the luscious flowers keep the mood firmly romantic.*

BELOW *Use different materials on the matching bedside lamps to prevent a scheme becoming boring.*

The romantic colour spectrum runs from shades of white through soft pastels and faded vintage hues to rich, dark jewel tones. Eye-poppingly bright shades can also work well in a romantic setting, especially when used for traditional or ornate pieces. A wall clad in tongue and groove, for example, can become an exciting focal point when painted a bright lime green, while simple wooden kitchen chairs suddenly have a whole new personality when sprayed neon pink. There are no limits to how much can be achieved with a simple tin of paint.

Combining colours in novel ways can also produce good results, especially when using shades that sit only a few degrees apart in the spectrum. Burnt oranges and deep pinks may seem offputting, but actually go really well together. Get inspired by looking through travel books — think of the pinks and oranges of Rajasthan or the riotous primaries of the clothing of Peru's indigenous people.

Pastels have of course always been a romantic staple, but after the pistachio greens and candyfloss pinks of the

RIGHT *The owner of this house found two framed pictures of flowers in a junk sale, then painted her own version to hang between them.*

OPPOSITE *The same background colour was used to paint the interior of an armoire, which really makes the items on the shelves stand out – even a motley collection of granny's old china would look great when displayed this way. Use loose covers on a sofa or chair to break up a strong colour scheme.*

BELOW *When showing off your vintage clothes and accessories, make sure the hangers are also worthy of the attention.*

Eighties, now pastels are of a slightly dirtier, more sophisticated variety, with underlying base notes of black and grey. This makes them easier to use in a living room or kitchen, while the more sugary versions can be reserved for the nursery.

Romantic whites are also more sophisticated than their brilliant white cousins. There are plenty of whites on the market now that fit into a traditional scheme, with base notes of grey for a Scandinavian feel or pinky-yellow for walls that reflect candle light beautifully – these go well in bathrooms and bedrooms, as they flatter your skin tones and make you look better naked.

Dark purples, greens and blues can work wonders in a romantic setting, but need a helping hand to stop them feeling gloomy. Plenty of

candlelight is vital, preferably arranged close to reflective surfaces such as mirrors or metallic accessories to maximize the available light. It's also wise to avoid heavy fabrics and cushions in a dark room, as you might otherwise end up with more of a Victorian smoking-room feel than the glamorous boudoir you envisaged.

If you are painting a room in a rich, jewel-like colour, an effective trick is to paint all the woodwork, including the skirting boards, window frames and even floors, in the same shade. Rather surprisingly, this actually creates a more uniform and spacious effect. The myth that small rooms should always be painted in a light colour must also be discounted, as a well-lit small space can look much more interesting when painted a rich colour rather than bland magnolia.

THIS PAGE *Dried flowers work well in a romantic setting, especially hydrangeas, whose petals change from blues and purples to the palest greys as they dry. A deep cerulean blue vase works well against the turquoise jewellery in the glass box.*

OPPOSITE ABOVE LEFT *Cups in saturated blues and burnt oranges decorate an open shelf. This style of crockery can often be found in French country kitchens.*

OPPOSITE ABOVE RIGHT *Dark hues create a sensual space, with plenty of pretty lights to lift the mood. The absence of fabrics and soft furnishings stops the room from becoming too heavy, and the mirror in the fireplace bounces light around.*

OPPOSITE BELOW LEFT *Ornately gilded mirrors create a marvellously glamorous room, and if the gilding is a bit scuffed, then so much the better.*

Without flowers and fabrics, the romantic home would be a dull place indeed. These two staples are the main mood setters for a cosy home, and add interest and freshness all year round. Vintage fabrics are an inexhaustible source of lovely patterns in muted, faded shades, and can be picked up cheaply. When it comes to flowers, think simplicity — a single sprig can have as much impact as a bunch of blooms and a loose posy looks better than a tight bouquet.

Flowers & fabrics

OPPOSITE *Vintage bedspreads and eiderdowns piled together make a lovely display. Have them professionally cleaned before use to restore colour and freshness. Store them in a glass-fronted cupboard so you can enjoy the patterns, even when they're packed away.*

ABOVE LEFT *Luscious roses are perhaps the ultimate bloom for romance. Here they create a temporary still life to delight the senses.*

ABOVE CENTRE *The watery greens and mellow pinks on these lovely cushions fit perfectly in a romantic scheme. Look for a common denominator*

when matching fabrics, whether it be a base note like the pinks above or a floral pattern.

ABOVE RIGHT *Flower displays look best when they're not too neat or contrived. Here, a handful of blooms spills out of an old jug for a pretty, cottagey effect.*

LEFT *These sugar-pink hydrangeas with their lush green leaves look extra delicate displayed in an antique metal container. Garden pots and planters work equally well indoors, and can easily be moved as the weather dictates.*

BELOW LEFT *An old glass jar is given a new lease of life as a vase, underlining the simple beauty of the flowers.*
OPPOSITE *This is romantic styling at its best — why opt for only one vase of flowers, when you can have many?*

If you are a lover of all things floral, soft and feminine, then this is an area where you can really give your leanings free rein. In a romantic home, blooms can appear in all shapes and forms, whether they be the fresh variety in vases or blowsily adorning furnishing fabrics and linens. Old-fashioned fabrics such as silk, lace and chiffon also find their natural place in a romantic home, and even damaged versions can sometimes be brought back to beautiful life with just a little bit of TLC.

When choosing flowers and plants to adorn your romantic home, remember the guiding rule: keep them simple, informal and loose. The look should be one of thrown-together bunches of hand-picked flowers freshly gathered from the garden, rather than something constructed or carefully arranged. Architectural arrangements and spiky combinations should be avoided at all cost – they look better in a pared-back, minimalist interior. Any flower that could have come from a cottage garden works beautifully in a romantic interior – roses, hydrangeas, anemones and peonies, for example, look ravishing when bunched together informally in vases, but remember to keep the stems short and the posies loose.

If you are lucky enough to have a garden, so much the better. Be creative when it comes to choosing which blooms to plant, as even weeds can have a strange beauty

of their own. Even if you don't have a garden, a few delicate, lofty stems of cow parsley cut from a country lane will look great in a vase on the mantelpiece, thanks to its intensely green hue and tiny white petals, while even a large bunch of bright dandelions can add to a vibrant colour scheme.

Also study the textures and shapes of foliage and other types of greenery. Trailing ivy looks great cascading from a bunch of flowers, while tender birch leaves, silky lilac foliage and ornamental grasses can lift a simple posy into something sublime. Twiggy herbs like lavender, thyme and rosemary will bring both structure and scent to an arrangement, and single twigs studded with berries or blossom look stunning displayed in sturdy jugs. Even the vegetable patch offers up visual delights – the deep purples of red cabbage and wispy carrot tops are beautiful in their own way and allow you to bring natural colour and texture into your home all year round.

Any vessel that can hold water can be used to house your floral delights, from a fine cut-crystal vase to a plastic jug. A group of empty milk bottles can house single roses, for example, while a glass jar could be filled with handfuls of wild flowers straight from the field. Flea markets, auction houses and car boot/yard sales are good hunting grounds for unusual vases – a vintage carafe that has lost its stopper can still offer a home to a sprig of cherry blossom, while a chipped teacup gets new life when filled with palest pink peonies.

OPPOSITE AND ABOVE *The deep, glossy purple of the cherries acts as a foil to the pink peonies – they are almost too beautiful to eat. Using an antique lace tablecloth lends an instant sense of occasion to even the simplest of tea parties. The bright pink chair gives a modern air to the room.*

Setting a beautiful table for tea with flowers, dainty china and a lace tablecloth could be said to sum up the romantic style perfectly – it's all about the small pleasures in life, whether that means spreading a freshly ironed cloth on the table or letting the smell of baking permeate your house. It can also be about using well-loved items in your home, either those you have inherited yourself or bought from a market or antiques store.

PREVIOUS PAGE LEFT Two very different floral arrangements give a relaxed look to a table. This is mirrored by the two mismatched chandeliers hanging from the ceiling – mixing things up lends a charming air of spontaneity to a room.

PREVIOUS PAGE RIGHT The smaller of the two arrangements displays vivid colour combinations, but it's hard to make flowers clash – they all tend to work well together. The glass is hand painted – an easy way to personalize inexpensive modern glassware.

ABOVE LEFT Old furnishing fabrics that are worn in places can be cut up and used to make smaller items such as cushions. Here, two vintage toiles are offset by a chunky corduroy.

ABOVE CENTRE A vintage silk dressing gown that is now too delicate to be worn can still be put on display or used as an adornment on a bed.

ABOVE RIGHT When you spot a piece of fabric that you love, buy it. You might not use it straightaway, but like these layered fabrics, it will be a thing of beauty in its own right.

Fabrics have a sensuality and appeal that might be hard to find in, for example, a mahogany chest, and they are also easy to vary to give different feels to your home. If you've never done it before, buying old textiles may feel daunting, especially if they are stained or have a slightly musty smell. But if you're attracted by a particular pattern or texture, try to overcome any qualms and buy the piece of fabric, as almost all problems can be overcome.

Pure linen is one of the hardiest fabrics there are, and ages beautifully, getting softer and softer as the years go by. Monogrammed linen sheets give a romantic look to a bed, and linen kitchen towels are super absorbent – they are also good for drying delicate glasses, as they shed hardly any fibres. Cotton is also tough, and can, like linen, be washed on high temperatures to get rid of any stains – after all, in the days before washing machines, cotton sheets and clothing used to be boiled to get them whiter than white.

Hand-embroidered pieces may be frayed and stitches may have come undone, but any

THIS PAGE *Whether it's the finest Chantilly or a rustic, crocheted variety, lace can be used all over the home. It's fairly easy to find in specialist vintage clothing shops, antiques stores or even charity shops/thrift stores. It lends itself particularly well to window covering, due to its transparent nature. So drop all thoughts of net curtains, and instead hang proper lace with pride. Small tablecloths can be turned into cushions, while scrap pieces of lace can be reworked into decorative throws or even stitched onto cotton and used as humble kitchen towels.*

self-respecting haberdashery department/notions store should be able to supply you with a spool of matching thread, and perhaps even show you how to replicate tricky stitches. You can also cut out any unaffected panels of embroidery and stitch them onto plain backgrounds to create cushions and quilts.

Lace comes in a variety of designs, from handwoven to machine-stitched pieces. If it has yellowed due to age or exposure to sun, give the piece an antique look by letting it soak in water and tea bags – the tannins in the tea will give a sepia tint to the material and conceal any light stains.

One of the best things about romantic style is that it allows you to show off the things you love. Take another look at your possessions — even the humblest items can be combined into an arresting display that is so much more than the sum of its parts. Whether your passion is for vintage china, old postcards or costume jewels, this section contains some pointers on how to create pleasing displays and maximize the impact of your treasures.

On display

OPPOSITE *It doesn't take much to create a romantic display in the kitchen — a selection of odd teacups, mismatched plates and cute mugs look great when grouped together in shelving made from recycled painted floorboards. The tongue and groove enhances the cottagey look.*

ABOVE LEFT *Can it get any more romantic than this? A boudoir-style vintage dressing table is heaped with sparkling accessories and delicate floral fabrics, and a pair of high-heeled beauties are left out to be admired rather than worn.*

ABOVE CENTRE *The delicate calligraphic curls of the wirework offset a collection of black and white images perfectly.*

ABOVE RIGHT *Create an Alice In Wonderland vibe by piling old silk lampshades on top of one another. Secure them with a stitch if necessary.*

Knick-knacks, bric-a-brac, fripperies – come on, you know you love them! For too long, ornaments have been dismissed as belonging only on the mantelpiece of old ladies' front rooms, but when used in the right way, they can really enhance a romantic room. The trick is to create a coherent theme with your treasures, whether they are linked by colour, pattern or a decorative style. It is also important to keep a sense of humour and to know when a collection looks cute and when it's simply over the top.

In most cases, more is better – if you're going to make a china collection a focal point, make sure there's plenty of it, instead of one

ABOVE *Team a vibrant lampshade with fresh roses in the same hue to bring interest to a simple scheme.*
RIGHT *Vintage bunting and flags can be found via specialist websites and stores, and add an instant hit both of colour and nostalgia. The paired wooden panels, wall lights and seaside paintings all bring a sense of structure and symmetry to an eclectic look.*

THIS PAGE *If you have magpie-like tendencies, there's no better way to display your treasured trinkets than on a dressmaker's dummy. Heap on necklaces, silk flowers, brooches, pins and rosettes to your heart's content and wrap fairy lights around the dummy for added sparkle.* **OPPOSITE** *An old tutu on a pretty hanger has been further adorned with a garland and fabric flowers. The wicker bust can also hold fresh blooms for a short time.*

forlorn matching tea set. By the same token, if you are hanging pictures, it will have greater effect if you hang them en masse rather than having a single isolated image above the sofa.

It can take time to assemble the most effective collections, especially if the items are vintage. Let's face it, buying 56 matching pieces of modern china from a department store, then showing them off on an open shelf is never going to have the same impact as a collection of pieces that have been carefully selected and lovingly brought together from a variety of antiques shops, flea markets and car-boot/yard sales over the years.

If your collection is two dimensional – framed photos or prints, for example – make sure you hang it on a calm, monochrome background to avoid a fussy look. And when it comes to framed images, it's fine to freely

THIS PAGE *These two floral images look all the better for being hung high on the wall, where they have plenty of breathing space. A tapestry chair sits well beneath.*
OPPOSITE FAR LEFT *Create your very own personal picture gallery on the stairs, showcasing the memories that matter. Lay out the pictures on the floor first to work out an arrangement that you're happy with.*
LEFT *A simple white bedroom is given personality thanks to a jumble of framed pictures on the wall.*

mix up photographs, drawings, postcards and paintings, but go easy on bright, modern holiday snaps to keep the look romantic.

If you want to impose some kind of order on a wall-hung display, create one or two straight lines – by lining up all the tops or the left-hand sides of the different frames, for example – then hang the rest of the images higgledy-piggledy inside. If you want your art collection to run up the stairs, hang pictures in your direct line of vision as you stand on a tread, so that you don't have to hover in mid-air when you look at them.

China, ceramics and glass are gratifyingly easy to find and make for fabulous displays. Go hunting in antiques shops, car boot/yard sales and charity shops/thrift stores for delicate porcelain teacups, cut-glass vases and ceramic bowls – the best thing is that mismatched items look even better than a matching set,

ABOVE AND BELOW *If you've got it, flaunt it. Mix up your mother's old china with finds from markets and charity shops / thrift stores to create a display that's all yours. Just remember to stick to a theme to give a coherent effect and avoid a chaotic or cluttered junk-shop look. A zesty colour behind the china makes it stand out and look fresh and modern.*
OPPOSITE *The rich, saturated colours of these cups and saucers makes the display hang together and look stunning.*

and it doesn't matter if the item is scratched or chipped – that just adds to the charm.

Don't forget to keep your chosen theme in mind when you're out buying, whether it be bold floral patterns or monochrome designs in deep jewel tones. Then you can mix up different eras, sizes and shapes for an eclectic-looking collection that is still somehow unified, either by colour or theme.

When displayed, your treasures will have much more impact when set against a bold backdrop. Paint the background wall or the inside of an old armoire in a funky modern shade, which will offset your china collection and bring it right up to date so that it looks fabulous rather than fusty. And make sure you choose the items with care – then all that dusting will be a true labour of love.

THIS PAGE *This softly pleated lampshade in a delicate chiffon-type fabric is just the right side of granny chic. The velvety texture of the blowsy garden roses adds a further hint of softness.*

When setting a romantic mood, lighting is key. Twinkling candlelight, soft shades and sparkling chandeliers improve the way your room looks and create an instant sense of relaxation. And helpfully, it's both an inexpensive and quick way of giving your home a stylish ambience. Just remember to keep your task lights and ceiling lamps bright, to stop you from fumbling around in the dark — with a few easy tips you can be both romantic and practical.

Lighting

ABOVE LEFT *Flickering tealights in antiqued mirror glass holders give off a gentle, evocative light that is perfect to illuminate a romantic meal or to bring a hint of glamour to bathtime.*

ABOVE CENTRE *This electric chandelier marries practicality with prettiness. As well as providing ambient overhead lighting, the delicately tinted glass droplets pick up the rich magenta of the walls and the delicate shades of the Indian-style prints.*

ABOVE RIGHT *Surrounding tealights with reflective sources such as mirrors, glass or metallic holders doubles the impact and creates a lovely glow.*

ABOVE LEFT *A vintage floorlamp is great for task lighting, and fits in with a romantic scheme. Try a good old-fashioned Anglepoise or a design classic from Jieldé, which work in all room settings.*

ABOVE RIGHT *If you are lucky enough to find an antique vanity mirror, grab it. For a similar effect, wrap mini lights or an LED chain around a circular modern mirror.*

You can have the most romantic home in the world, but if you don't get the lighting right, you really won't do it justice – vintage furniture looks old and worn under a brutal striplight, while if highlighted with shaded table lights and clusters of tealights it will take on a beautifully nostalgic look.

The gentle, flattering tones of candlelight immediately spring to mind when thinking of a romantic interior. You can use candles in tall candelabras for a dinner party, to highlight a nice corner of a room, or displayed in a variety of single glass holders.

There are also chunky pillar candles, which make an impact clustered in a grate or on a mirrored tray – just make sure you leave a space between the candles, as if they are allowed to melt together and create one giant puddle of wax, they give out an enormous amount of heat and can become a fire hazard.

Tealights are incredibly versatile and inexpensive. You can show them off in all kinds of containers, from glass jars to teacups, as long as they are heat resistant – use the same kind of creative thinking as you would when looking for containers for flowers.

THIS PAGE *To soften up an all-white room scheme, pile on the candles. Spread them out throughout the room, from church candles in the fireplace to a full-blown chandelier and scattered tealights. Having plenty of mirrors in a white room also increases the brightness, bouncing light around and really making the most of the candlelight. Paint all the mirror frames white to keep the look coherent.*

THIS PAGE *Doubling up your candelabras is a clever romantic styling trick – it loosens the overall look and keeps it eclectic. By combining candles with electric lights you also get two very different sources of light, one for ambience and one for functionality. Display the candles alongside flowers and fruit for added impact.*

OPPOSITE *Twinkling chandeliers above and flickering tealights below create a magical setting. Using plenty of different holders for the tealights creates a quirky feel, and keeps the table fun.*

Strings of decorative mini lights have moved away from the Christmas tree and little girls' bedrooms to offer an easy and inexpensive way to light up your life. Most chain stores with a lighting department carry unusual, pretty strings of lights adorned with stars, flowers, chillies, diamonds and more. Drape them on picture frames, twine them around iron bedsteads, bunch them up in glass vases or wrap them around mirrors for a hint of sparkle.

With their delicate, sparkling charms,

chandeliers epitomize romantic style and have become increasingly popular in the past few years. They come in all shapes and sizes and at every price point too. There are plenty of modern reproductions on the market – many home furnishing stores offer pretty electric chandeliers that look brilliant in a romantic home. However, for the romantic style it's better to opt for a vintage vibe if possible.

The main trick with tealights is to use plenty of them. There is nothing more forlorn

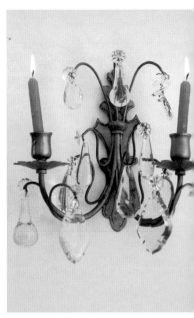

CLOCKWISE FROM TOP LEFT *Make a feature of a lovely old teacup and saucer. Candlemaking kits can be sourced online and make perfect gifts. Collect glass candlesticks in different heights and shapes, and place brightly coloured candles in them for pretty effect. You could also use metal candlesticks, like pewter, silver or brass, but make sure they are dull and aged rather than new and shiny. The*

mantelpiece is the perfect home for candles, and when they are placed in front of a mirror their effect is doubled. Use coloured candles in a traditional sconce for a modern look. A string of mini lights looks great heaped around a scented candle. Single-stem flowers take on a whole new life when lit from below with tealights — the warmth of the flames also releases their scent.

OPPOSITE *Use different types of candles on a dinner table to create a romantic look. The slender mercury-glass candlesticks illuminate the food from above and throw atmospheric shadows, while the tealights light up the intricate petalled heads of the hydrangeas.*

than a single tealight on a dinner table – more is definitely better. You don't need to match all the containers, quite the opposite – a varied array of holders will make for a much nicer, quirkier effect.

Scented candles have become ubiquitous in recent years, and their delicious perfumes can cause great impact in a room. A hot bath surrounded by fragrant Diptyque candles is utter bliss, while a Jo Malone version is a staple on many bedside tables – scented candles can even help you work better if you light one in your home office. The one room they should not be used in is the kitchen, at least not while cooking or eating – having a strong scent of camellia or roses hovering while cooking a roast can create a knock-out olfactory effect, but not in a good way.

If you are after a genuine antique and are prepared to pay for it, there are plenty of

antiques dealers that specialize in chandeliers and who will also come and hang one for you (make sure you have a ceiling strong enough to hold it first). But for most of us, flea markets and car-boot/yard sales are the best starting points. The old chandeliers that you may find here will probably be missing a drop or two, but in a romantic scheme this slightly worn effect is desirable anyway. Make up for any missing parts by mixing in mismatching drops from a different chandelier. These can often be found in antiques or junk stores and the droplets can also look great on thin chains or ribbons, suspended in a row in a window. You can also customize your chandelier further by adding ribbons, feathered birds and butterflies, silk flowers or strings of pearls – anything that takes your fancy. If you opt for a vintage chandelier, it's important that you get an electrician to take a look at it before you hang it – it may need to be rewired for safety.

Flea markets and junk stores are also treasure troves when it comes to old table lamps and lampshades. Don't be scared to mix a base you like with a shade from somewhere else; just keep the proportions in mind. If you are handy with a sewing machine, picking up the wire base for a shade is cheap and easy, then you can customize it with whatever fabric you have at hand. For a cute look, invest in a length of bobbled braid or long fringing from a good haberdashers/notions store and stitch it all along the edge of the shade. Once again, a sense of fun adds so much personality to a romantic scheme.

OPPOSITE, CLOCKWISE FROM TOP LEFT, *Chandeliers can pull a romantic scheme together, and come in all shapes, sizes and styles. These are all vintage, but new varieties can look just as good. The delicate rose-tinted example would look* great in a bedroom, while clear glass droplets work equally well in a hallway and a living room. If you find a slightly too traditional chandelier, customize it with ribbons, feathers, beads or, as here, with tiny paper birds. You can also change some of the drops for a truly bespoke version.

THIS PAGE Lampshades are an easy way to prettify a room. Choose a vintage example with slightly shabby good looks, or make your own using an old wire frame.

Romantic rooms

THIS PAGE *Romantic decorative touches can work wonders in even the most modern of kitchens.* **OPPOSITE** *The focal point in this kitchen is the eclectic shelving, constructed from reclaimed floorboards. To focus attention on this feature, the work surfaces and other units have been kept deliberately simple and understated, although a subtle layer of texture has been added to the central island by tiling the sides.*

Cooking & eating

Preparing and sharing food is one of the most rewarding things in life, and the kitchen is often described as the heart of the home. Creating a soulful atmosphere here is a labour of love, and the aim is to create a space that is warm, inviting and friendly — perfect for rustling up a quick supper or entertaining friends over leisurely dinners. Plan your kitchen carefully so that it fills all the practical criteria, then when it comes to the decor give your romantic creativity free rein.

Modern families tend to spend a lot of time in the kitchen — as well as a space for preparing food, cooking and eating there, the kitchen also plays host to myriad other activities such as entertaining, homework, internet browsing, working from home, TV viewing and socializing. So it's important that this hub of activity fills two criteria: it needs to be both useful and beautiful.

The romantic style tends towards the sweetly nostalgic with retro hints, but there's no reason to let a passion for the past affect the functionality of your kitchen — you really don't want to hang onto an old-fashioned cooker, an energy-inefficient fridge or a set of blunt knives just because they happen to be vintage. Quite the opposite in fact, and even the sleekest contemporary stainless-steel kitchen can be given a pretty romantic twist.

If your kitchen is modern in style, there are a few easy ways to introduce romantic elements. Cladding the walls with tongue and groove will create a clean-cut cottage style, which works well even in new-build houses due to the linear vertical effect created by the grooves. The look

LEFT *A romantic look can be simple and utilitarian too, enhanced by retro accessories such as this poster. The metal bread bin and other metallic touches add a dash of glamour, while glimmering tealights set the mood. The single garden rose is the perfect romantic finishing touch.*

ABOVE *Stacked Moroccan tea glasses add an exotic note to a pared-down white kitchen, thanks to their jewel-like hues and richly gilded patterns.*

manages to be both modern and retro at the same time, and the surface can easily be painted in durable paints that are suitable for kitchens.

Tiles are also great for an easy and relatively inexpensive update, but steer clear of patterned tiles with motifs of vegetables or fruits – they smack more of the 1970s than romantic style. Instead, look for textured tiles, which create a gently rustic effect. Tiles in deep, lustrous hues are also a good way of adding a colourful element to plain walls. If you only want to tile a small area – behind the stove or the kitchen sink, for example – you can opt for more expensive tiles, as you need a relatively small amount. Shimmering mosaic tiles are often confined to bathrooms, but they can work

equally well in kitchens. You could also consider using mirrored tiles, as they reflect the light so beautifully.

If you go for an eclectic kitchen with lots of decorative detail, keep the backdrop simple and pared back. Avoid brash primary colours and instead aim for softer shades with neutral undertones. Pale greens work well, as do greys, whites and blues. Hits of colour can then be added in the shape of china, flowers and textiles, which are easy to change or move around as the mood takes you. Even dark walls – racing-car green or elephant grey – can work well in a kitchen, as long as you get the lighting right to ensure a well-illuminated yet still romantic atmosphere.

THIS PAGE *An all-white dining room is thoroughly relaxing. The French-style chairs work well with the simple, chunky dining table and luscious garden roses create a ravishing focal point.*

LEFT *Simple, rustic and beautiful – this kitchen works on many levels and is a fairly easy look to achieve. The tongue and groove pulls the eye upwards, away from the plentiful under-counter storage. The vases filled with fresh blooms bring the outdoors in, and a vintage kitchen towel adds colour. The salvaged brass tap is positioned quite high on the wall to showcase its beautiful shape. Purple and pink candles in a metal candelabra add the finishing touch.*

RIGHT *Doubling up chandeliers is a good styling trick that creates a relaxed, quirkily romantic mood. The tiny tealights shimmer on the table and their flattering glow makes the food (and guests!) look great, while fresh flowers provide colour and scent.*

CLOCKWISE FROM TOP LEFT *Single vintage plates and odd pieces of glassware make for a charmingly eclectic table and can be sourced from car boot / yard sales or flea markets. These dainty knives and forks with acrylic handles in boiled sweet / hard candy shades*

make a lovely display, as they are all the same shape yet the jewel colours ring the changes. Tempting, colourful food can also lift a table setting, so think about how it will look as well as taste when you plan your menus. Despite the different patterns and

sizes, these stacked plates picked up from a variety of places look great together — it's the gold detailing they have in common that ties them all together. When placed handles up in a tureen, this cutlery / flatware creates the same effect as a bunch of flowers.

Storage is key in any cooking zone, and the trick in the romantic kitchen is to have a hardworking combination of closed cupboards and drawers, and open shelves. Kitchen gadgets such as juicers or food processors are rarely objects of beauty, so make sure they are stashed away when not in use. On the other hand, elegant wine glasses and decorative vintage tea sets should be displayed with pride on open shelves. The thought of dusting may seem daunting, but if you only have items that you use frequently on display, they won't have time to gather dust. Be ruthless when you select your things, and only keep the best-loved and prettiest objects in sight.

If you choose plate racks or a shelving system where kitchenware is permanently on display, make sure that worksurfaces are kept clear of clutter. Certain things you'll need to have out, such as a toaster or a kettle, but other kitchenalia can be put away in drawers

ABOVE *Hide appliances behind panels of vintage fabric, adding some pattern in the process. Antique storage jars bring order to surfaces.* **LEFT** *Shelves stacked higgledy-piggledy with china and tableware should look a mess, but the chunky shelves and cupboard painted in a soothing shade bring harmony to the scheme.*

or hung up on walls. It's important to plan plenty of storage space for items such as stationery, computer leads and phone chargers, and bills and paperwork. This ensures that your kitchen feels more like a welcoming haven than a stress-inducing scrapheap.

Lighting in a kitchen is obviously important so that you can tell the difference between chopping a carrot and your little finger. But once the task lighting is sorted, it's equally important to remember mood lighting. Cute wall lights can jazz up plain walls, vintage table lamps look good on sideboards or the end of a run of worksurfaces and chandeliers take pride of place over a dining table. Try to fit a dimmer switch for a chandelier so that you can turn it up full when you want to sweep up crumbs under the table, then turn it down romantically low for dinner a deux. And, of course, candles are invaluable, not only on the kitchen table at dinnertime but also dotted throughout the space. Why not intersperse cups and plates displayed on shelves with twinkling tealights to highlight their patterns?

A romantic table is one that delights all the senses, from sight to smell via touch and taste. Just remember rule number one when it comes to romantic styling: never match too exactly, sticking to a theme instead. At its most simple, a theme can be a single colour in a range of different shades – pinks ranging from powder to magenta, for example, or greens varying from pistachio to jade. Vintage plates and heirloom tea sets are, of course, your first choice, but there are also plenty of shops that sell stunning tableware in modern but pretty hues.

Glassware is an important part of the romantic table too. Drinking glasses can be of all sizes and shapes, as long as you find them beautiful. Old decanters are brilliant for adding sparkling cut-glass style, while pressed-glass jugs in jewel shades add a pretty edge.

TOP *A wall-mounted plate rack has been painted the same colour as the kitchen units and holds riotously patterned plates.* **ABOVE** *A selection of inherited and bought china adorns a kitchen shelf. If you have fallen in love with a specific pattern, china-matching websites such as chinafinders.com can trace a make and manufacturer so that you can top up your collection.*

Textiles can be used in many different ways – as table decorations, or in a more practical fashion. If you come across vintage fabric in an antiques shop, snap it up. It might not be enough to upholster a chair, but if you want to hide an unsightly washing machine or dishwasher in your kitchen, there is no better way than to sew a simple panel and hang it in front of the appliance. You could also cut fabric into smaller squares and hem it to use as napkins. If you love the fabric enough to look at it every day, then creating a splashback is an original idea. Have a piece of heat-resistant glass cut to size and back the fabric onto it for a personal style statement (this also works brilliantly with wallpaper).

Lace instantly adds a romantic note, and can be used to great effect in a kitchen or dining area. Place a layer of lace atop a colourful tablecloth for a layered effect, or back pieces onto strong cotton to make a lovely kitchen towel. If you find large scraps of

ABOVE *Dark-coloured kitchens can be deeply romantic, provided the lighting is both adequate and mood enhancing. If background colours are dark, you can use white accents like these candelabras and the chairs to great effect.*
OPPOSITE *Black tiles and a black chandelier create a sultry ambiance that works surprisingly well in this kitchen. The ornate frame used to hold a mirror, but was painted a bright white and is now displayed purely for its own decorative impact.*

lace, stretch them across wooden frames and place them in the window to create an update on net curtains, or just loosely stitch them into a panel that lets the light through but stops passersby from seeing in.

The type of food you serve will also set the right mood. A traditional afternoon tea with tiny sandwiches and cakes served on a dainty stand is about as delightful as it gets, but more substantial meals can also look stunning. Think about the colours of the food when you plan the menu, as well as the flavours – plates of palest-pink prawns offset with tender green asparagus are a visual feast, while dainty glass sundae dishes heaped with rounded scoops of ice cream and glistening berries will delight adults and kids alike.

THIS PAGE *Play with light in dark kitchens for a sultry, sensuous space. Here, the walls are raw polished concrete with dark units to match, but the overall effect is exciting rather than gloomy. The large chandelier is a dramatic focal point and reflects light from other sources as well. Pots, pans, toaster and appliances are all in sparkling stainless steel, to bounce light around.*

OPPOSITE *The majestic chandelier is enhanced by opulent decorative touches. The metal-clad dining chairs reflect the various light sources, which include candles and strands of mini lights.*

Living

From elegant salon to relaxed family den, the living room
has to play many different roles. We entertain in it,
watch television, hang out as a family, read and play.
But most of all the living room is a place to relax in,
which makes it a great backdrop for romantic style. Fill it
with flowers, cushions, candles, table lamps and pictures
to create a space that really reflects your personality.
With good storage facilities to hide away technology and
clutter, this can become a room to fall in love with.

ABOVE *A beautifully
tranquil spot for a quiet
cup of tea. A scattering of
plump cushions provides
comfort on the simple
ironwork sofa, while
delicate lace panels allow
the sunlight to filter in.*
OPPOSITE *A fairly simple
living room with modern
lines has been given hits of
romance in the shape of
embroidered floral
cushions and the imposing
bouquet on the table. The
long shagpile rug creates
interest on the floor and
offsets the sleek wood-
panelled walls.*

If you have a family or live with a partner, the style of the living room can become a bone of contention. Bedrooms, bathrooms and even kitchens lend themselves easily to romantic style, but the living room is the one place in the house where everybody's differing needs and wishes come together and need to be taken into account. Marrying your romantic vision with the kids' gaming consoles and the husband's giant plasma screen might not be easy, but it can be done.

If you have a house big enough to separate the screen-based activities – television watching, game-playing – into a different room, then your problems are solved. Keep the sitting room technology free, and dedicate it to civilized pursuits such as reading and entertaining; the way a living room used to be – a place to sit back and relax in after a long day, a place set aside for the gentle arts of conversation, reading and crafting.

Most of us, though, have to meld all these things together in one space. And that's where clever storage comes in. Avoid modern storage systems and look for beautiful antiques instead, such as old French armoires or wooden wardrobes. A carpenter can easily convert the insides to hold a plasma screen or DVD player, while digital viewing boxes and game consoles can be stashed away in the drawers at the bottom. Capacious rattan containers or big round baskets can hold joysticks and cabling, while DVDs can be neatly stacked away in sideboards or chests.

ABOVE *Make a feature of magazines by stacking them neatly under a Perspex / Plexiglass table.*
OPPOSITE *A neutral scheme is enlivened by a stunning rug by Marni from The Rug Company. The red and pink tones are picked up in the cushions, while girly dresses hanging from the mirror prettify the room.*

If you can't find suitable pieces of furniture, some companies specialize in fitting sliding panels on the wall to completely conceal plasma or flat screens. You could also hang large paintings in a pattern around the screen to camouflage it slightly.

Books tend to gather in living rooms. Go through your library, choose the most beautiful volumes and display them on a coffee table, or stack them on a side table with some candlesticks and a mirror for a lovely display.

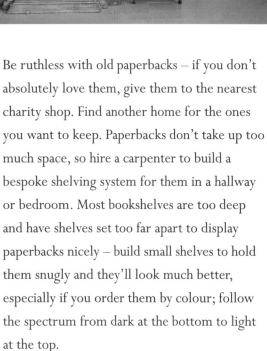

LEFT *Modern art can work well in a romantic room. Here, the wall sconces have been given edge with pink candles.*

BELOW *Placing a lamp in front of a mirror doubles the effect. Bunches of flowers also look twice as lovely when reflected.*

Be ruthless with old paperbacks – if you don't absolutely love them, give them to the nearest charity shop. Find another home for the ones you want to keep. Paperbacks don't take up too much space, so hire a carpenter to build a bespoke shelving system for them in a hallway or bedroom. Most bookshelves are too deep and have shelves set too far apart to display paperbacks nicely – build small shelves to hold them snugly and they'll look much better, especially if you order them by colour; follow the spectrum from dark at the bottom to light at the top.

A fireplace is, of course, the perfect focal point for a romantic living room. Log-burning stoves are increasingly popular thanks to the Scandinavian stoves now available, which are reasonably priced and heat the room very effectively, as well as scoring high on the environmentally friendly list. Gas fires are now also better looking than the old-fashioned versions, and nowadays there are also flueless fires that create a cosy ambience but don't need a chimney. If you have a fireplace but no fire, use a string of fairy lights or a selection of pillar candles to create a flame-like effect.

RIGHT *Bright pinks create a friendly, inviting glow in this living room. You can use a strong colour throughout — even on upholstery and furniture — for maximum impact in an interior. The table in the middle of the grouping is higher than the average coffee table, but is perfect for keen card players.*

OPPOSITE *The lovely wooden floorboards in this house are really given the chance to shine. The high windows are another great asset — the shocking pink curtains are actually saris from India that the owner hung as a temporary measure when she moved in, but loved so much that they're still there.*

A mantelpiece is the perfect place to express your romantic creativity. A large, ornate mirror in a gold frame will reflect candles and flowers placed in front of it beautifully, and doubles the impact of your favourite ceramics or other knick-knacks.

The sofa tends to be the hub of a living room. Far too often it's positioned directly opposite the television and effectively prevents the room from being a place for socializing, quiet reading and playing games. If you can conceal the television, so much the better, but you could also opt for sofas and chairs on castors that can be moved around easily. There is no law that says the sofa has to be pushed up against a wall. If your room is big enough, group the furniture in the middle and use the walls for shelves and storage, or prop up a huge mirror or an ornate empty frame. The perfect arrangement would be one or two sofas and a combination of

LEFT *A light, airy room filled with books and antiques creates a feeling reminiscent of a manor house library.*

ABOVE *The symmetry of the lights and the intricate ironwork chairs make this quite a strict room, but the neutral shades and tactile fabrics create a relaxed feel.*

upholstered armchairs facing each other in a group that invites conversation. It's amazing how the formation of our rooms shapes our behaviour – if you have sofas and chairs facing each other over a table, the chances that someone will break out the Scrabble are far higher than if you all sit staring at the TV.

Sofas and armchairs are also perfect repositories for that most romantic of items, the decorative cushion. From floral motifs to sleek silks, there is really no limit to how many you can pile on the sofa, as long as you leave yourself space enough to sit. Cushions are also an easy, quick way of updating a room or ringing the seasonal changes. In winter time you can plump for cushions in darker, deeper shades and heavier materials, such as velvet, brocade and chintz, while the summer months are better

suited to lighter colours and cotton, silk and satin fabrics.

Curtains are another way to freshen up your space. In winter we all feel like shutting the darkness out and cocooning behind heavy drapes, while when spring comes our spirits lift as easily as a light voile curtain fluttering in the breeze. Don't be afraid to use vintage curtains, as they are ready made and cut the considerable costs of having new ones made. Buy slightly overlong ones, then go hunting for tasselled tiebacks, or get creative and make your own with feathers, pearls and beads. To avoid the overall effect being overly traditional or heavy, just tie the curtains back to one side, rather than parting them in the middle.

Lighter fabrics don't require elaborate rails and hanging systems. Stitch flat loops to the top of the curtains, or buy large metal eyelets to punch through the curtain heading, then thread onto a rod. Stretched lace, net or chiffon panels can also work well, as they let

in plenty of daylight while maintaining some privacy. Roman blinds in unstructured linen are ideal for a pared-down effect, while simple wooden shutters make a good backdrop for a romantic room scheme.

Floors should be kept natural where possible. Check out your existing floorboards to see if they can be sanded and varnished, or lay real wooden flooring. Extra-wide boards look very elegant and create a great sense of space. They are available in shades from dark ebony to bleached birch whites. Natural flooring such as sisal and jute also looks good, as it has an easy, casual feel that offsets busy floral patterns on cushions and textiles. Avoid fitted carpets, which can look too traditional in a busy room with lots of pattern.

Rugs add both texture and colour and can really pull a room together. If you opt for a simple monochrome design, make sure that it adds interest in terms of texture – long, looped strands, perhaps, or an unusual weave. A boldly patterned floral rug can be stunning, but check that it doesn't clash with the other textiles – after all, this is supposed to be a room for relaxing in.

Lighting can make or break the mood in any room. Avoid a single pendant light in the middle of the room and instead spread your light sources evenly throughout the space. Don't forget that you'll need task lighting positioned wherever you intend to read or work. In addition, place pretty decorative table lamps on as many surfaces as possible, from occasional tables to sideboards, or even on the floor. Uplighters, in the shape of floorstanding lights with pretty silk shades or dramatic gilt wall sconces, create the impression of higher ceilings, and dimmable lights are essential for when you just require a low level of light to complement a flickering fire or lots of twinkling candles.

OPPOSITE *This room proves that perfection should not always be sought after. The walls are untreated cement and plaster —a look that the owner fell in love with when renovation work was taking place. So she decided to leave them untreated, and instead painted the cornicing and ceilings an interesting duck-egg blue. The shade is echoed in the elaborate chest of drawers, which provides a glamorous focal point.*

THIS PAGE *The colour scheme in the room was inspired by the painting, which the owner has always loved. The scuffed state of the frames and walls adds charm and soul to the room. The deep gold and bronze tones are picked up in cushions and throws on the sofa. The metal wire sculptures on the wall were sourced in Mexico.*

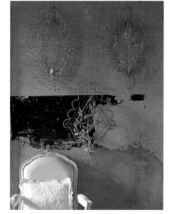

OPPOSITE *A vintage lace tablecloth has been used to great effect as a bedspread. In an all-white bedroom, use plenty of textures — lace, fringes and fur — to create interest. The mirrors keep the room light and airy.*

RIGHT *A dainty mirrored console table makes the perfect dressing table or writing desk in front of the window.*

BELOW *Scatter sweet touches around the room, such as these lavender-filled fabric hearts.*

Sleeping

Muted tones, tactile fabrics, glittering jewels and plenty of blooms all come together to create a romantic bedroom. We spend a third of our lives asleep, and need a soothing haven to help us reach that state. And waking up in beautiful surroundings also helps ease you into the day. The bedroom is your most intimate space, one where you can cast off the stresses of the day, so make it the most personal room in the house and let your love of romance blossom.

Your bedroom should be your favourite place in the whole world, a soothing hideaway where you can let go of all the tensions of the day and rest both body and soul. Other areas of the house have to be shared with family and friends and are a showcase for visitors and guests, but the bedroom is yours and yours alone. So don't feel restricted by style diktats or passing trends – instead, decorate and furnish this most private of retreats in colours and patterns that you love and which feel right for you.

The main item of furniture in the bedroom is, of course, the bed, and it's also one of the most important items in your home. It's remarkable how many people will spend a small fortune on a sofa, but still sleep every night on a lumpy old mattress. A good rule is to invest as much as you can in a good mattress.

A surprising number of people buy beds and mattresses online, without trying them out first. It's vital that you go to a selection of showrooms and department stores to research which type best suits you. And don't stand next to the bed feebly pressing a hand down on it to test it – discard your inhibitions and lie down in your preferred sleeping position for a trial run.

There is a plethora of mattress types on the market, from simple sprung examples to foam-topped, hand-stitched versions. A good mattress should last you up to 10 years, so it's crucial to get it right – you'll be surprised how much more rested and relaxed you'll feel after a night in a good bed.

Once you have chosen the right mattress, you can start thinking about a bed frame. Four-poster beds are ideal for the romantic look, as are carved or upholstered French beds. Antique versions are very sought after and therefore expensive, but modern reproductions can look equally glamorous. Upholstered headboards have made a comeback in recent years, but they are a far cry from the 1960s kitsch salmon faux-velvet versions. Modern upholstered headboards are oversized, sometimes reaching all the way to the ceiling, and covered in sumptuous silks, sleek leather or bold patterns. For a simpler version, buy tall MDF boards and stretch your favourite fabric tightly over them (stapling it in place on the back), then just place the boards flush with the wall behind the bed.

ABOVE AND RIGHT *Moroccan sequinned fabric covers this headboard – a good tip if you're bored of your bed frame. Lingerie in sorbet shades looks good enough to eat hanging from a carved screen.*
OPPOSITE *A girly boudoir is a wonderful place to spend some downtime. Powder pink hues keep the mood serene.*

OPPOSITE ABOVE LEFT *An antique chair piled with linens, books and jewels is a charming still life.*
OPPOSITE ABOVE RIGHT *You might not wear your grandmother's pearls, but you can still enjoy their lustre by displaying them on a vintage plate. Brooches and fabric flowers add extra glamour.*

OPPOSITE BELOW LEFT *Some clothes are just too pretty to be hidden away in a wardrobe. Make them into artworks by showing them off on pretty hangers.*
OPPOSITE BELOW RIGHT *Antique clutches might not be practical for everyday use, but make perfect romantic bedroom accessories.*

THIS PAGE *The soft coral tones in this room create a soothing mood and are flattering for bare skin. Candlelight is always good for keeping romance alive. If you find a beautifully upholstered bed like this, let it take centre stage in the room and keep other furniture to a minimum.*

Bedroom walls are the obvious place for some of the many romantic floral wallpapers that are on the market now. Don't be scared of using large patterns in a small room – a tiny, dense pattern will actually make a room feel even smaller, while big, bold patterns will open up the space. A wallpapered 'feature' wall, especially behind the bed, works well in a bedroom, and you should be able to afford more expensive wallpaper, as you don't need a large amount of it. Paint the other walls in a colour that complements the wallpaper.

Even if you are a sound sleeper, there will be times when you lie awake staring at the wall. The only solution to this problem is to make sure you have something worth looking at, whether it be personal photographs, framed drawings or other mementos that put happy thoughts in your head before you fall asleep. You can also add interesting touches to the ceiling. Some trendy hotels and restaurants are now wallpapering ceilings but leaving walls plain below high dado rails. Alternatively, wall stencils, which have become immensely popular in recent years, also work equally well on ceilings – they are particularly good for kids' rooms, to help the little ones nod off.

ABOVE AND RIGHT *A three-part mirror has been placed on a small dressing table to create a pretty still life with fresh flowers and old photographs. That most classic of perfumes, Chanel No 5, adds style to the setting.* **FAR RIGHT** *This antique screen is a perfect place to show off treasures. Vintage clothing can be a work of art when properly displayed.*

A beautiful piece of vintage fabric adorns this bedstead, while a another length has been draped across the bed. You could also achieve this look by building a simple frame behind the bed to hang fabric from. The grand lampshades on either side are given a quirky makeover with two different bases — romantic style is all about surprise and fun.

The bedroom is one of the few rooms where carpet really works, as there's not much through traffic and it feels pleasant beneath bare feet. If you head down the wall-to-wall carpet route though, don't use the space under your bed for storage, as carpet traps dust and you'll need access to hoover regularly. Soft rugs and animal skins cast on plain wooden floorboards are also pleasing underfoot, especially sheepskins and shagpiles.

If you read in bed, you'll need a good bedside light. Again, hotels are good sources of inspiration, as they provide a selection of lighting sources beside the bed. Choose a directable lamp to read by, but also keep a pretty table lamp on your bedside table for mood lighting. Make sure that all the bedroom lights can be switched off from the bed, as having to jump out of a warm bed to switch off the lights is not a good feeling. Scented candles and tealights also create a luxurious mood and can set a romantic scene — just don't fall asleep without blowing them out.

Bed linen creates great impact and can be easily changed to create different moods. Be realistic when you think of how you make your bed – are you the type who takes the time to lovingly plump, puff and layer bedspreads, throws and cushions every morning, or do you just want to shake the duvet about a little? Then choose according to your findings. If you are the layering type, make sure you have somewhere to store the cushions and covers when they come off – a blanket box at the end of the bed is ideal for this, and also creates a good spot to sit and put your clothes on. There

RIGHT *Pay attention to small details such as pretty doorknobs. They come in all shapes, sizes and colours and are great ways to freshen up a room without breaking the bank.* BELOW *Even if you only have a tiny nook, you can use treasured pieces to create a romantic still life that will inspire you in the morning.*

are such beautiful duvet covers on the market now that you can get away with a simple version as well, plus just a couple of decorative cushions for effect.

Make sure your wardrobe is big enough to keep all your clothes tucked away, but leave some of your most beautiful pieces out on display. Your best-looking shoes can also be left out to be admired – what's the point of having Manolos and hiding them away? And that's what your romantic bedroom should be all about – being near to the things you love.

OPPOSITE *Pages from an old portfolio of botanical prints have been given new life as pictures in simple modern white frames. Note that the pictures have not been* *hung symmetrically, but fitted around the shape of the bed. The carved roses on the bed are mirrored in the cushions and in a hanging fabric rose on the bed knob.*

THIS PAGE *Introduce vintage touches in unexpected ways. Here, a kitsch nude, a metal hostess trolley and an upholstered armchair create a lovely bathing space.*

Bathing

As far as physical pleasures go, bathing must surely be one of the top contenders. And the bathroom is somewhere you can really give your romantic side free rein — showering might be quick and functional, but for that special treat, there's nothing like sinking into a deep bubble bath in a room filled with candles, aromatic potions and beautiful things. Aim to stimulate all your senses and pay attention to even the smallest details to make the bathroom the most sensual of all the rooms in your home.

ABOVE LEFT *Fresh flowers and pretty scented soaps create a still life to enjoy every day. Make sure less attractive toiletries and cleaning products are tucked away out of sight.*
ABOVE RIGHT *If you have the space, incorporating furniture that does not traditionally belong in a bathroom is a great way to create a relaxed room where you'll want to linger. This mirrored wardrobe makes the bathroom into a dressing room too.*

For the ultimate sensory bathing experience, filling the tub with hot water isn't quite enough. You need to surround yourself with things that you love, from scents to textures to sounds. No matter how big or small it is, your bathroom can transport you to the land of your dreams.

We all fantasize about a huge bathroom with a freestanding tub standing proudly in the middle of the room, preferably in front of a fireplace. Some people have adopted the idea of having a bathtub in the bedroom – a look that was first sported by cool luxe hotels – but for

most of us, the reality is a fairly standard-sized room that usually has to be shared with our partner and kids.

However, no matter how small your space, there are plenty of ways to transform your bathroom into a tranquil oasis. For a romantic look, you can't beat a roll-top or slipper bathtub. If your budget stretches far enough, you could buy a proper cast-iron tub in your chosen colour (but you'll need to check that your floor is strong enough to carry a tub like this first). More wallet-friendly reproduction

THIS PAGE *If you have high ceilings, use subway-style tiles to halfway up the wall, then add a dado or a peg rail to create interest, as large expanses of bare white wall can look clinical. Opt for larger tiles on the floor to increase the sense of space in the room.*

OPPOSITE *In older properties, a box room could be converted into a dream bathroom rather than becoming a repository for junk. Alternatively, you could create the perfect bathing space in an airy loft conversion, or in an extension to the master bedroom.*

CLOCKWISE FROM ABOVE LEFT *Even the smallest details are important in a room that should be dedicated to relaxation and beauty. Singing in the bath is more fun if you have access to your favourite music — choose a retro-style radio that matches the romantic mood.*

If you have artistic talents, buy glass paint and decorate a simple mirror with some delicate, old-fashioned motifs. Salvaged doorknobs add some soul to a modern bathroom. Soaps that look good enough to eat should be displayed. Show off the most beautiful of your toiletries.

antique-style tubs can also be found at discount bathroom retailers. Salvage yards are also worth investigating for old baths, but do make sure you sit down in them to try them out before buying – you'd be surprised how narrow-hipped the Victorians were.

Vintage basins can work well even in new houses, and most bathroom-fitting companies sell taps/faucets that look suitably retro. But most importance should be placed on accessories, such as mirrors, tiles, hooks and shelves.

Tiles can instantly transform a bathroom, and are worth spending both time and money on. Give the ubiquitous square white tiles a miss, and instead open your eyes to the enormous variety there is on the market. Rectangular subway-style tiles are easy to track down, while individual vintage tiles can be found at flea markets, antiques markets and car boot/yard

LEFT *Be bold and cover a whole wall with a mural or dramatic wallpaper. A curtain tassel serves as a light pull, and round glass lamps make shaving and applying make-up a breeze.*
BELOW *Create a pretty and unusual toilet paper holder by threading crystal beads onto strong thread or thin wire, then suspend from a hook in the ceiling.*
OPPOSITE *Using large mirrors in the bathroom really opens up the space, as they double the light. Incorporate flowers into the room as natural air fresheners. Think of the bathroom as any other room in the house, where you would hang pictures, display mementos and show off pretty clothes, and plan clever storage to hold all the boring necessities as well.*

sales, then used to create a completely bespoke splashback behind the basin.

Mirrors are all too often banished to their designated space above the basin, but try cladding two of the walls in mirror to open up the space and maximize light. Antique, gilded frames or cut-glass mirrors are both stunning and light reflective, but modern versions are now widely available as well – just mix them up with a few vintage pieces to create an authentic romantic look.

Equally important is lighting. No matter how gorgeous you are, we all have those mornings when we dread seeing our face in the mirror,

and good lighting can help with this. As with the rest of your home, you will need several different varieties of light, such as mood lighting, task lighting and overhead lighting. A chandelier can look fantastic in a bathroom, but before hanging one check with an electrician that it's suitable for damp and humid environments. Task lights either side of a mirror will help with shaving and applying make-up. Keep lamps simple and effective, or go for showgirl glamour with a light bulb-encircled mirror. Candles are good for creating mood and both candlesticks and candelabras look good in a romantic bathroom.

When you buy flowers for your home, don't just concentrate on the living or dining room. Your bathroom also deserves a few blooms – even a stem or two will look great if placed in a window or by the mirror. Plenty of potted plants thrive in bathrooms too, due to the humidity, and if you have a south-facing window this might well be the best place in the house for exotic or tropical plants.

Towels add both colour and texture, and are an easy way to ring the decorative changes. Gone are the days when the height of luxury was a bath sheet in beige towelling to go with your minimalist white tub. Nowadays, there is a riot of colours and patterns available, from psychedelic stripes to simple hammam towels with slinky fringing. In fact, using a thin towel (rather than the deep-pile terry towelling

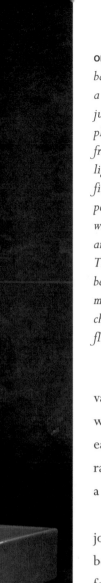

OPPOSITE *Dark bathrooms can have a very sensuous feel — just remember to install plenty of light sources, from ambient to task lighting. The exciting finish on these walls is polished concrete, which creates a tactile and durable surface. The grey tones are beautifully offset by metallic hints, and change visibly in flickering candlelight.*

LEFT *Keep the sanitaryware and taps modern for an edgy look.* **RIGHT** *A laser-cut wooden screen makes an effective window treatment, while the chiffon kimono lets the sunlight filter through beautifully.* **BELOW RIGHT** *Crystal, cut glass, diamanté and lace are combined to glamorous effect. Recreate this look in a little nook or on a shelf.*

variety) is a good idea, as cotton and linen will absorb the water from your body easier and also dry quicker on the towel rail – perhaps save the plush towelling for a snug dressing gown instead.

Decluttering the bathroom is an essential job. Medicines, pots and potions should all be tucked away in a cabinet – keep only a few specially chosen decorative items out on display. Decant your shampoos and shower gels from their plastic containers into pretty glass jars and bottles – you'll be surprised how effective the look can be.

Pretty soaps can also be shown off to great effect. Either group them together in a shallow dish or pile them into a large glass vase. Look out for unusual and colourful examples in distinctive wrapping when you are abroad, to bring an exotic note to your bathroom.

A country garden is the epitome of romantic style. Roses, peonies, abundant tender green leaves, birdsong and afternoon tea under a parasol make for an abundance of romance in the air. You can recreate this atmosphere no matter how small your outdoor space and whether it's deep in the country or in the heart of the city.

Outdoors

OPPOSITE *This idyllic scene can be recreated with a selection of garden chairs, a parasol, an armful of flowers and some simple tableware — all you need to complete the scene is the sun.* **ABOVE LEFT** *Create a container garden using classic terracotta pots or old planters and fill them with scented white lilies, bay trees and trailing ivy.* **LEFT** *Mismatched pieces of lace create a pretty, impromptu tablecloth. Keep the tableware simple and relaxed, and extend this theme to the food you serve — think rustic bread, cheese and juicy summer fruits.*

RIGHT *Even the smallest garden can be a secluded hideaway with some clever planting. Wire arches can carry scented climbers such as jasmine and honeysuckle. Simple deckchairs are perfect for a rest from gardening – the frames can be bought cheaply and the fabric seats are easy to sew from your own choice of upholstery material.*
OPPOSITE *This Indian parasol is a thing of beauty in its own right, with its bold magenta lining and jangling metal fringe.*

We've all read in glossy interiors magazines about bringing the outside in, but this chapter is all about doing exactly the opposite – bringing the inside out. Throw caution to the wind and pretend that there is no such thing as a rainy summer by moving your favourite cushions, linens, tableware and furniture outside. Pile pillows high on a sun lounger, drag your favourite reading chair into a place in the sun and, if you're really yearning to go back to nature, carry your bed into the garden for all-day lounging.

There is no reason for preparing for outdoor entertaining in any other way than you would an indoor dinner party. As soon as the sun comes out, the shops sport gaudy plastic plates and garish glasses that are supposedly better suited for alfresco eating than your normal china.

There are obvious reasons for using unbreakable items when on a beach or having a picnic in the park, but if you are planning to treat your family and friends to a dinner in the garden or on a balcony, bring out your most loved and beautiful tableware. Few things are as civilized as sitting in a shady nook on a gorgeous summer's day at a properly set table complete with a white cloth, clinking cutlery and cold white wine in elegant glasses.

If the weather is beautiful, allow yourself to enjoy it. Put down the washing, lawn mower or whatever you have at hand, bring out some cushions and just relax into the moment. Even a simple cup of tea beneath a gently swaying canopy of branches can become a memory strong enough to carry you through the winter months to come.

If you're lucky enough to have the space for a verandah or expanse of decking that's under cover, you can extend the summer by sitting outside whether it's sunny or showery. Even a small canopy, like the type you take camping, is worth investing in for those days when the weather can't quite make up its mind.

THIS PAGE *Clothes that have dried in the sunlight exude a scent no fabric softener can mimic. If you can hang your clothes close to scented rosebushes, so much the better, or try drying lavender to scatter in your chest of drawers.*
OPPOSITE *Who wouldn't want to spend a summer's evening on a verandah such as this one? With its all-white scheme, from the clapperboard to the wooden seats to the bunting, it's a supremely inviting space. For your own version, string up outdoor fairy lights and make up bunting in your favourite fabric — for a rainproof version, use oil cloth.*

Keep evening chills at bay by supplying your guests with fleecy blankets. It might not sound like the most elegant of scenes, but in Scandinavian cities outdoor bars and restaurants offer them to guests as soon as evening comes, and sometimes whole piazzas and pedestrianized streets are filled with people keeping warm and toasty beneath Ikea blankets. If this is not enough, buy scented wood and fill up your barbecue – a blazing fire always keeps the cold at bay.

Whatever the size of your outdoor space, two things will make it feel instantly like an outside room: adequate seating and proper lighting. Even a balcony can be transformed into a magical spot with the help of a bistro table, a couple of chairs and some twinkling outdoor fairy lights to add seductive sparkle to summer nights.

For bigger gardens, invest in lamps that can light up interesting trees and bushes – place them at the end of the garden to draw the eye there at night, making your outside space seem more spacious. Combine garden lights with solar-powered lights along a track, perhaps a backlit water feature and plenty of mood lighting, from storm lanterns to simple tealights in glass holders.

Modern garden furniture in heavy wood or metal can be cumbersome, expensive and definitely not romantic. Instead, take inspiration from past times and far-flung

OPPOSITE AND ABOVE RIGHT
A Moroccan-style tea party is a great way to entertain friends. This shelter was quickly erected from tall bamboo canes, which can be bought in garden centres. Then a length of fabric was thrown across, filtering the sun and creating a tent-like effect.

RIGHT *For the ultimate in summer indulgence, drag a bed into the garden. A Victorian cast-iron bed can be painted in rustproof paint or even spray-painted like a car to stop it from rusting in the rain. Just remember to bring the bedding in when it starts spitting.*

LEFT *Many lovely items from inside your home can be brought into the sunshine for special occasions. Fill a whole tree with twinkling chandeliers, storm lanterns and hanging tealights, and place a small table underneath for dinner for two — use your coffee table and some rugs for a laid-back feast.* **OPPOSITE** *Create your own sanctuary with a vintage sun lounger, a fluffy eiderdown and some cushions. Now all you need is a good book, a jug/pitcher of iced tea and your phone set to silent.*

places. Delicate wrought-iron Victorian and Edwardian benches, tables and containers will pretty up any space, as will colonial-style rattan seating, while low-level cushions and pouffes from Morocco and Thailand add an exotic touch and invite you to lounge on lush summer lawns. If you are worried about the effects of rain and dew, there are plenty of outdoor fabrics that are created to withstand humidity, or you could opt for oil cloth – companies like Cath Kidston and Marimekko offer designs that range from cute polka dots to blowsy blooms.

There are many more ways of entertaining in your garden than the conventional barbecue. Throw a proper cocktail party with glimmering chandeliers and tealights hanging in the branches of a tree or suspended on strong string attached along garden fences. Hold an afternoon tea party with all the trimmings, from cucumber sandwiches to clotted cream atop freshly baked scones. Alternatively, just drop a frozen strawberry into a glass of white wine, sip it outside and revel in your very own romantic haven.

Sources

Selina Lake
Interior Stylist
+44 (0)7971 447785
www.selinalake.co.uk
www.selinalake.blogspot.com
@selinalake

An Angel at My Table
www.anangelatmytable.co.uk
Wooden kitchens and furniture.

Anna French
www.annafrench.co.uk
Wild Flora wallpapers
and fabrics.

Anthropologie
www.anthropologie.eu
Romantic linens, tableware
and accessories.

Chic Shack
77 Lower Richmond Road
London SW15 1ET
+44 (0)20 8785 7777
www.chicshack.net
Painted furniture and accessories.

The Cloth House
www.clothhouse.com
Fabrics from around the world.

Cole and Son
10 Chelsea Harbour
DesignCentre
Lots Road
London SW10 0XE
www.cole-and-son.com
Find hand-printed wallpapers.

David Austin Roses
www.davidaustinroses.co.uk
English garden roses available as
plants and cut flowers.

**Decorative Country
Living**
www.decorativecountryliving.
com
Antique French mirrors,
chandeliers and furniture.

Elena Deshmukh
www.elenadeshmukh.com
Beautiful hand-embroidered
cards.

Farrow & Ball
www.farrow-ball.com
Heritage paint colours.

**The French Bedroom
Company**
www.thefrenchbedroom.com
Beds and furniture with a
romantic French feel.

Graham and Green
4 Elgin Crescent
London W11 2HX
+44 (0)20 7243 8908
www.grahamandgreen.co.uk
Visit the website for details of
their other stores.
Large range of furniture and
accessories from around the world
plus lighting, all available to
order online.

**The Indian Garden
Company**
www.indiangarden
company.co.uk
Raj-style garden parasols
and garden accessories.

Keep Calm Gallery
47 Jennings Road
East Dulwich
London SE22 9JU
+44 (0)20 8480 0022
www.keepcalmgallery.com
Framed screen prints, cards and
tea towels.

Lavender Room
16 Bond Street
North Laine
Brighton BN1 1RD
+44 (0)1273 731039
www.lavender-room.co.uk
Romantic homeware, gifts, clothes
and accessories.

Lisbeth Dahl
www.lisbethdahl.dk
Pretty glassware, candles, cushions
and accessories.

Louise Body Wallprint
www.louisebodywallprint.com
Wallpaper, cushions and fabrics.

Nest Pretty Things
www.nestprettythings.com
Gorgeous charm jewellery.

Osborne and Little
www.osborneandlittle.com
Fabrics and wallpapers.

Powder Blue
3–5 Francis Street
Leicester LE2 2BE
+44 (0)116 270 3303
www.powder-blue.co.uk
French furniture and romantic
homewares, accessories and gifts.

**The Real Flower
Company**
+44 (0)1730 818300
www.realflowers.com
Fragrant garden roses and herb
bouquets by post.

Roberts Radio
www.robertsradio.co.uk
Iconic 1950s-style retro radios in
various pastel shades.

Royal Doulton
www.royaldoulton.com
Pretty plates, teacups
and saucers.

The Rug Company
124 Holland Park Avenue
London W11 4UE
+44 (0)20 7229 5148
www.rugcompany.info
High quality rugs by many
famous designers.

Sunbury Antiques
Kempton Park Racecourse
Staines Road
East Sunbury on Thames
Middlesex TW16 5AQ
www.sunburyantiques.
com
Furniture, vintage plates,
eiderdowns and textiles. Market
days on second and last Tuesday of
each month from 7am–2pm.

Tine K Home
www.tinekhome.dk
Danish online shop selling
stylish homeware.

Unique Coat Hangers
www.uniquecoathangers.
co.uk
Large selection of fabric padded
clothes hangers.

UV Centre
+44 (0)20 8123 5530
www.uvcentre.com
Pink neon furniture paint

Zara Home
www.zarahome.com
Pretty bath towels, bed linen,
cushions and tableware.

US SOURCES

ABC Carpet & Home
888 & 881 Broadway
New York, NY 10003
(+1) 212 473 3000
Visit www.abchome.com
for details of a retail outlet
near you.
*Handmade dinnerware, vintage
pieces, soft silk pillows and dainty
wrought-iron chandeliers.*

Anthropologie
www.anthropologie.com
*Floral wallpaper and murals,
pastel toile de Jouy pillows, pretty
white tableware and flowery
bed linen, all with vintage
romantic charm.*

Bauer Pottery
www.bauerpottery.com
*Richly colored vintage style
dinner- and tableware.*

Bella Notte Linens
www.bellanottelinens.com
*Romantic bed linen and pillows
in sumptuous fabrics.*

Cowtan & Tout
(+1) 212 647 6900
www.cowtan.com
*Home furnishing fabrics in
romantic prints from Colefax
and Fowler, Cowtan & Tout, Jane
Churchill, Larsen and
Manuel Canovas.*

Charles P. Rogers
55 West 17th Street
New York, NY 10011
(+1) 212 675 4400
www.charlesprogers.com
*Romantic brass and iron bed
frames, along with wooden
sleigh beds.*

Dress My Shade
www.etsy.com/shop/
dressmyshade
*Vintage-style lampshades
with decorative trims.*

Fishs Eddy
889 Broadway
New York, NY 10003
(+1) 212 420 9020
Call 1 877 347 4733 or visit
www.fishseddy.com for their
other two store locations.
*Pretty glassware with delicate
etched floral patterns as well as
cake stands and dainty toile-
printed serveware.*

Garnet Hill
www.garnethill.com
*Bedding, linens and home
accessories.*

Hoyle Lamps
Lamp Shades & Lamps Outlet
2233 East Main St.
Lincolnton, NC 28092
(+1) 704 732 8001
www.hoylelamps.com
*Antique fringed silk lampshades
and hand-painted hurricane
lamps as well as some
reproduction pieces.*

IKEA
www.ikea.com/us
*Some well-priced romantic-style
pieces including chandeliers,
simple four-poster beds and
floral linens.*

Laura Ashley
www.lauraashley-usa.com
*English-garden-look floral,
striped, checked and solid cotton
fabrics for every room in the
house. Also furniture, accessories
and lighting.*

Mombasa Net Canopies
www.mombasabrand.com
*Romantic bed hangings made
from mosquito netting.*

Not Too Shabby
www.notooshabby.com
*Shabby chic and romantic-style
furniture, lighting (including
crystal chandeliers), rugs
and fabrics.*

The Paris Apartment
www.theparisapartment.com
*French boudoir furniture, mirrors,
bed linen, lampshades,
chandeliers, dressing room screens
and accessories.*

Pierre Deux
(+1) 212 570 9343
www.pierredeux.com
*Furniture inspired by romantic
French country style. Also
wallpaper, fabric and rugs.*

Remains Lighting
130 West 28th Street
New York, NY 10001
(+1) 212 675 8051
www.remains.com
*Reproduction and antique crystal
chandeliers and sconces.*

Salamandre Silk, Inc.
979 Third Avenue
New York, NY 10022
(+1) 212 980 3888
www.scalamandre.com
Reproductions of classic fabrics.

Secondhand Rose
138 Duane Street
New York, NY 10013
(+1) 212 393 9002
www.secondhandrose.com
*Huge collection of vintage
wallpapers from Victorian
to 1970s.*

Thibaut
480 Frelinghuysen Avenue
Newark, NJ 07114
(+1) 800 223 0704
www.thibautdesign.com
*Glorious floral textiles
and wallpaper.*

Vintage Chic Furniture
www.etsy.com/shop/
VintageChicFurniture
*Custom-painted antique furniture
and vintage decorative items.*

Woven Accents
525 North La Cienega
Boulevard
Los Angeles, CA 90048
(+1) 310 652 6520
www.wovenonline.com
*Antique and new handwoven
rugs and tapestries.*

Picture credits

1 The home of Debbie Johnson, owner of Powder Blue; 2–4 Available for location hire at www.shootspaces.com; 5 above centre Available for location hire at www.shootspaces.com; 5 above right The home of Jenny Atherton, co-owner of Lavender Room in Brighton; 5 below left The home of Ros Fairman in London; 5 below centre Available for location hire at www.shootspaces.com; 5 below right The home of Rosie Harrison co-owner of www.aandrphotographic.co.uk and www. airspaces.co.uk; 6–7 Available for location hire at www.shootspaces.com; 8–13 The home of Ros Fairman in London; 14–15 The home of Debbie Johnson, owner of Powder Blue; 16 Bed of Flowers, B&B owned by Floriene Bosch www.bedofflowers.nl; 17 above and left The home of Carol McKeown, owner of Baby Ceylon; 17 below The family home of the artist Sharon Tzortzi www.sharontzortzi.com; 18 Bed of Flowers, B&B owned by Floriene Bosch www.bedofflowers.nl; 19 below The family home of the artist Sharon Tzortzi www.sharontzortzi.com; 20 left The home of.Rosie Harrison co-owner of www.aandrphotographic.co.uk and www.airspaces.co.uk; 20–21 The family home of Maria and Gary Myers, founders and owners of Chic Shack www.chicshack.net; 22–23 The family home of Nicky Sanderson, the co-owner of Lavender Room in Brighton, East Sussex; 24. The home of Debbie Johnson, owner of Powder Blue; 25 The family home of Nicky Sanderson, the co-owner of Lavender Room in Brighton, East Sussex; 27 The family home of Maria and Gary Myers, founders and owners of Chic Shack www.chicshack.net; 28–29 The London home of Tracey Boyd and Adrian Wright; 30 left The family home of the artist Sharon Tzortzi www.sharontzortzi.com; 30–33 The London home of Rebecca Hill of French Country Living; 34 above The home of Rosie Harrison co-owner of www.aandrphotographic.co.uk and www.airspaces.co.uk; 34 below Available for location hire at www.shootspaces.com; 35–37 The home of Debbie Johnson, owner of Powder Blue; 38 The family home of Nicky Sanderson, the co-owner of Lavender Room in Brighton, East Sussex; 39 above The home of Jenny Atherton, co-owner of Lavender Room in Brighton; 39 below The home of Debbie Johnson, owner of Powder Blue; 40–41 The London home of designer Kathy Dalwood (www.kathydalwood.com) and artist Justin Mortimer (www.justinmortimer.co.uk); 42 The home of Carol McKeown, owner of Baby Ceylon; 43 The home of Rosie Harrison co-owner of www.aandrphotographic.co.uk and www.airspaces.co.uk; 44 The family home of Maria and Gary Myers, founders and owners of Chic Shack www.chicshack.net; 46 above Bed of Flowers, B&B owned by Floriene Bosch www.bedofflowers.nl; 46 below Available for location hire at www.shootspaces.com; 47 The London home of designer Kathy Dalwood (www.kathydalwood.com) and artist Justin Mortimer (www.justinmortimer.co.uk); 48–49 The home of Debbie Johnson, owner of Powder Blue; 51 left and right Available for location hire at www.shootspaces.com; 52 above left The family home of Nicky Sanderson, the co-owner of Lavender Room in Brighton, East Sussex; 52 above centre The home of Rosie Harrison co-owner of www.aandrphotographic.co.uk and www.airspaces.co.uk; 52 above right and below left. The home of Debbie Johnson, owner of Powder Blue; 52 below centre The home of Jenny Atherton, co-owner of Lavender Room in Brighton; 52 below right The London home of Rebecca Hill of French Country Living; 53 The home of Debbie Johnson, owner of Powder Blue; 54–56 Bed of Flowers, B&B owned by Floriene Bosch www.bedofflowers.nl; 57 Available for location hire at www.shootspaces.com; 58 and 59 above Bed of Flowers, B&B owned by Floriene Bosch www.bedofflowers.nl; 59 below Available for location hire at www.shootspaces.com; 60 above left The London home of designer Kathy Dalwood (www.kathydalwood.com) and artist Justin Mortimer (www.justinmortimer.co.uk); 60 above right and below left The family home of the artist Sharon Tzortzi www.sharontzortzi.com; 61 The home of Jenny Atherton, co-owner of Lavender Room in Brighton; 62 Available for location hire at www.shootspaces.com; 63 left The home of Rosie Harrison co-owner of www.aandrphotographic.co.uk and www.airspaces.co.uk; 63 centre The home of Carol McKeown, owner of Baby Ceylon; 63 right Available for location hire at www.shootspaces.com; 64 above The home of Ros Fairman in London; 64 below The family home of Nicky Sanderson, the. co-owner of Lavender Room in Brighton, East Sussex; 65 The family home of Maria and Gary Myers, founders and owners. of Chic Shack www.chicshack.net; 66–67 The London home of designer Kathy Dalwood (www.kathydalwood.com) and artist Justin Mortimer (www.justinmortimer.co.uk); 68–69 Bed of Flowers, B&B owned by Floriene Bosch www.bedofflowers.nl; 70 left The London home of designer Kathy Dalwood (www.kathydalwood.com)

and artist Justin Mortimer (www.justinmortimer.co.uk); **70 centre** The home of Carol McKeown, owner of Baby Ceylon; **71 above** The home of Ros Fairman in London; **71 below left** The family home of Nicky Sanderson, the co-owner of Lavender Room in Brighton, East Sussex; **71 below centre** The home of Jenny Atherton, co-owner of Lavender Room in Brighton; **71 below right** The home of Debbie Johnson, owner of Powder Blue; **72** Available for location hire at www.shootspaces.com; **73 left and right** The home of Ros Fairman in London; **73 centre** The family home of Nicky Sanderson, the co-owner of Lavender Room in Brighton, East Sussex; **74 left** The London home of designer Kathy Dalwood (www.kathydalwood.com) and artist Justin Mortimer (www.justinmortimer.co.uk); **74–76** The home of Ros Fairman in London; **77** The home of Rosie Harrison co-owner of www.aandrphotographic.co.uk and www.airspaces.co.uk;. **78 left** The family home of Nicky Sanderson, the co-owner of Lavender Room in Brighton, East Sussex; **78–80** The London home of designer Kathy Dalwood (www.kathydalwood.com) and artist Justin Mortimer (www.justinmortimer.co.uk); **81** Bed of Flowers, B&B owned by Floriene Bosch www.bedofflowers.nl;. **82** The home of Carol McKeown, owner of Baby Ceylon; **83 left** The London home of Rebecca Hill of French Country Living;. **83 centre** The home of Carol McKeown, owner of Baby Ceylon; **84 left** The London home of Rebecca Hill of French Country Living; **84 right** The London home of Tracey Boyd and Adrian Wright; **85** The family home of Maria and Gary Myers, founders and owners of Chic Shack www.chicshack.net; **86–87** Bed of Flowers, B&B owned by Floriene Bosch www.bedofflowers.nl;. **88 above left and right** The home of Jenny Atherton,. co-owner of Lavender Room in Brighton; **88 above** centre The London home of designer Kathy Dalwood (www.kathydalwood.com) and artist Justin Mortimer (www.justinmortimer.co.uk); **88 below left** Bed of Flowers, B&B owned by Floriene Bosch www.bedofflowers.nl; **88 below centre** The family home of the artist Sharon Tzortzi www.sharontzortzi.com; **88 below right** The London home of designer Kathy Dalwood (www.kathydalwood.com) and artist Justin Mortimer (www.justinmortimer.co.uk); **89** The London home of Rebecca Hill of French Country Living; **90 above left centre** The home of Carol McKeown, owner of Baby Ceylon; **90 above right and below left** The family home of Nicky Sanderson, the co-owner of Lavender Room in Brighton, East Sussex; **90 below right** Bed of Flowers, B&B owned by Floriene Bosch www.bedofflowers.nl; **91 above** The home of Debbie Johnson, owner of Powder Blue; **91 below** The London home of designer Kathy Dalwood (www.kathydalwood.com) and artist Justin Mortimer (www.justinmortimer.co.uk); **92–93** The home of Rosie Harrison co-owner of www.aandrphotographic.co.uk and www.airspaces.co.uk; **94–97** Available for location hire at www.shootspaces.com; **98** The home of Jenny Atherton, co-owner of Lavender Room in Brighton; **99** The family home of Maria and Gary Myers, founders and owners of Chic Shack www.chicshack.net; **100–101** Bed of Flowers, B&B owned by Floriene Bosch www.bedofflowers.nl; **102–103** The London home of Tracey Boyd and Adrian Wright; **104–105** The home of Debbie Johnson, owner of Powder Blue; **106–107** The family home of the artist Sharon Tzortzi www.sharontzortzi.com; **108** Available for location hire at www.shootspaces.com;

109 The London home of Tracey Boyd and Adrian Wright; **112–113** The London home of designer Kathy Dalwood (www.kathydalwood.com) and artist Justin Mortimer (www.justinmortimer.co.uk); **114** The family home of the artist Sharon Tzortzi www.sharontzortzi.com; **115** Bed of Flowers, B&B owned by Floriene Bosch www.bedofflowers.nl; **116 left** The London home of Rebecca Hill of French Country Living; **116 right** and **117** The home of Debbie Johnson, owner of Powder Blue; **118–119** The home of Ros Fairman in London; **120–121** The home of Debbie Johnson, owner of Powder Blue; **122–123** The family home of Nicky Sanderson, the co-owner of Lavender Room in Brighton, East Sussex; **124** Available for location hire at www.shootspaces.com; **125** The home of Rosie Harrison co-owner of www.aandrphotographic.co.uk and www.airspaces.co.uk; **126 and 127 above** The home of Carol McKeown, owner of Baby Ceylon; **127 below** The home of Jenny Atherton, co-owner of Lavender Room in Brighton; **128 above left and below right** The home of Debbie Johnson, owner of Powder Blue; **128 above right** and **129** Available for location hire at www.shootspaces.com; **130–131** The home of Ros Fairman in London; **132 above** The home of Jenny Atherton, co-owner of Lavender Room in Brighton; **132 below** and **133** The London home of Tracey Boyd and Adrian Wright; **134–135** The home of Ros Fairman in London; **136** The home of Rosie Harrison co-owner of www.aandrphotographic.co.uk and www.airspaces.co.uk; **137** The family home of Maria and Gary Myers, founders and owners of Chic Shack www.chicshack.net; **138** The home of Rosie Harrison co-owner of www.aandrphotographic.co.uk and www.airspaces.co.uk; **139 above left** The home of Ros Fairman in London; **139 above centre and below centre** The home of Rosie Harrison co-owner of www.aandrphotographic.co.uk and www.airspaces.co.uk; **139 above right** The family home of Nicky Sanderson, the co-owner of Lavender Room in Brighton, East Sussex; **139 below right** The London home of Tracey Boyd and Adrian Wright; **140 left** The London home of designer Kathy Dalwood (www.kathydalwood.com) and artist Justin Mortimer (www.justinmortimer.co.uk); **140 right** The family home of the artist Sharon Tzortzi www.sharontzortzi.com; **141** The home of Carol McKeown, owner of Baby Ceylon; **142–143 left** The family home of the artist Sharon Tzortzi www.sharontzortzi.com; **143 above right** The home of Jenny Atherton, co-owner of Lavender Room in Brighton; **143 below right** Available for location hire at www.shootspaces.com; **144–145** The home of Debbie Johnson, owner of Powder Blue; **146** The home of Carol McKeown, owner of Baby Ceylon; **147** The home of Debbie Johnson, owner of Powder Blue; **148 above** Available for location hire at www.shootspaces.com; **148 below** The London home of designer Kathy Dalwood (www.kathydalwood.com) and artist Justin Mortimer (www.justinmortimer.co.uk); **149** The family home of Maria and Gary Myers, founders and owners of Chic Shack www.chicshack.net; **150–153** Available for location hire at www.shootspaces.com; **155** The home of Ros Fairman in London; **157** The home of Debbie Johnson, owner of Powder Blue; **160** The London home of Tracey Boyd and Adrian Wright.

Business credits

Floriene Bosch
Bed of Flowers B&B
Dijk 45
6641 LA Beuningen
The Netherlands
T: +31 (0)24 675 0849
M: +31 (0)1307 1489
E: info@bedofflowers.nl
www.bedofflowers.nl
Pages 16; 18; 46 above; 54–56;
58 and 59 above; 68–69; 81;
86–87; 88 below left; 90 below
right; 100–101; 115

Tracey Boyd
www.traceyboyd.com
Pages 28–29; 84 right;
102–103; 109; 132 below; 133;
139 below left; 160
Maroc Star rug in sitting
room (pp. 28–29) by Tracey
Boyd for Knots Rugs
563–565 Battersea Park Road
London SW11 3BL
T: 020 7228 2424
www.knotrugs.co.uk
White lacquer desk in sitting
room (28–29) by Tracey Boyd
for H.J.Contracts.
Contact: Wayne Morgan
HJCFurniture@btconnect.
com
43B Hardingham Road
Hingam
Norfolk NR9 4LX
T: + 44 (0)1953 851448
M: + 44 (0)7949 851470

Kathy Dalwood
www.kathydalwood.com
www.justinmortimer.co.uk
Pages 40–41; 47; 60 above left;
66– 67; 70 left; 74 left; 78–80;
88 above centre; and below right;
91 below; 112–113; 140 left;
148 below.

Ros Fairman
Location available through
www.airspaces.co.uk and 1st
Option Agency.
Pages 5 below left; 8–13; 64
above; 71 above; 73 left and
right; 74–76; 118–119;
130–131; 134–135; 139 above
left; 155

Rosie Harrison
www.aandrphotographic.co.uk
info@aandrphotographic.co.uk
T: +44 (0)20 7607 3030
and www.airspaces.co.uk
info@airspaces.co.uk
T: +44 (0)20 7607 2202
F: +44 (0)20 7607 2190
Pages 5 below right; 20 left; 34
above; 43; 52 above centre; 63
left; 77; 92–93; 125; 136; 138;
139 above centre and below
centre
Mural in bedroom by Brian
Ayling
T: +44 (0)20 8802 9853
Pages 34 above; 52 above centre;
92–93; 125.

Rosie also has a house to
rent in Essaouira, Morocco
www.atlanticmorocco.
com

Rebecca Hill
French Country Living
www.frenchcountryliving
antiques.com
E: f.c.l.com@wanadoo.fr
UK:T: +44 (0)7770
520 371
France:T:
+33 4 93 75 63 03
Pages 30–33; 52 below right; 83
left; 84 left; 89; 116 left.

Debbie Johnson
Powder Blue
3–5 Francis Street
Stoneygate
Leicestershire LE2 2BE
T: +44 (0)116 270 3303
www.powder-blue.co.uk
Eclectic mix of period and
contemporary furniture,
mirrors, chandeliers,
household and garden items.
Pages 1; 14–15; 24; 35–37; 39
below; 48–49; 52 above right
and below left; 53; 71 below
right; 91 above; 104–105; 116
right; 117; 120–121; 128 above
left; 144–145; 147; 157

Carol McKeown
Baby Ceylon womenswear
Unit 12 Portobello Green
Arcade
281 Portobello Road
London W10 5TZ
T: +44 (0)20 8968 9501
and at
11 Topsfield Parade
Crouch End
London N8 8PR
T: +44 (0)20 8348 5245
www.babyceylon.com
Pages 17 above and left;
42; 63 centre; 70 centre;
82; 83 centre; 90 above left; 126;
127 above; 141; 146

Maria Myers
Chic Shack
Furniture and home
accessories
77 Lower Richmond Road
London SW15 1ET
T: +44 (0)20 8785 7777
www.chicshack.net
Pages 20–21; 27; 44; 65; 85;
99; 137; 149

**Nicky Sanderson
and Jenny Atherton**
Co-owners of Lavender Room
16 Bond Street
Brighton
East Sussex BN1 1RD
T: +44(0)1273 220 380
www.lavender-room.co.uk
Pages 5 above right; 22–23; 25;
38; 39 above; 52 above left; 52
below; 61; 64 below; 71 below left
and centre; 73 centre; 78 left; 88
above left and right; 90 above
right and below left; 98;
122–123; 127 below; 132
above; 139 above right;
143 above.

Debi Treloar
Location available through
www.shootspaces.com
Pages 2–4; 5 above and below
centre; 6–7; 34 below;
46 below; 51 left and right; 57;
59 below; 62; 63 right; 72;
94–97; 108; 124; 128 above
right; 129; 143 below right;
148 above; 150–153

Sharon Tzortzi
www.sharontzortzi.com
Pages 17 below; 19 below;
30 left; 60 above right and below
left; 88 below centre; 106–107;
114; 140 right; 142–143 left

Index

Acknowledgments

Firstly, a massive thank you to Debi Treloar for taking such stunning photographs, and for being great company on all our shoot days…I love working with you!

Thanks to everyone who welcomed us into their inspiring and romantic homes – it was a pleasure to meet such interesting and lovely people. Also a big thank you to everyone involved with this project at Ryland Peters & Small, including Alison Starling for commissioning my Romantic idea, and Megan Smith, Jess Walton and Annabel Morgan. Plus thanks to my friends, in particular Gemsy, for always making me laugh, and to the lovely people who have featured my work on their websites and blogs – I really appreciate your support. Finally many thanks to Sara Norrman for putting *Romantic Style* into such beautiful words, plus a very special thanks to The Real Flower Company for their amazing bouquets.

And last but not least, my family. Thank you to my wonderful parents, Ronald and Valerie Lake for all your love and support – none of this would be possible without you both. Thanks to my sister Aimee for her encouragement and finally to my husband Dave – I love you.

Selina Lake

Eng... ...se Nylons